SO-AUN-298

*A Book for Women . . .
and the Men Who Want
to Love Them Better*

Delicious Sex

Gael Greene

PRENTICE HALL PRESS · NEW YORK

Acknowledgments

My special thanks to
Dr. Mathilde Krim
Dr. David Ostrow
Dr. Martin Schecter
Dr. Niels Lauersen
Eileen Grigg and Jamie Gillis
my editor, Phil Pochoda
Don Congdon, who championed this celebration of sex
and Mildred Newman, for her wisdom and insight

Text copyright © 1986 by Gael Greene
Illustrations (pages iii, 7, 12–13, 15, 22, 35, 58, 68, 80, 137, 163, and 174)
© 1986 by Dave Calver
Illustrations (pages xi and 75) © 1986 by Bill Russell

All rights reserved, including the right of reproduction
in whole or in part in any form.

Published by Prentice Hall Press
A Division of Simon & Schuster, Inc.
Gulf+Western Building
One Gulf+Western Plaza
New York, NY   10023

PRENTICE HALL PRESS is a trademark of Simon & Schuster, Inc.

Manufactured in the United States of America

With Love
to All the Wonderful Men
Who Taught Me Everything I Know
About Sex

Contents

Contents

The Author's Pledge

Listening to our poets, novelists, and songwriters, one would guess we are a culture that prizes love. And yet few of us devote nearly enough time or thought to making love. Too often sex is our last priority—after the kids are tucked in and the garbage is carried out for the night, or after an excess of margaritas has blurred our senses. That is why I have interrupted my usual work—reviewing restaurants and writing novels —to create this practical text.

Imagine. In just months, even weeks, you can discover a new level of sexuality. You will be happier in your body, sexier in your brain, more fun (and having more fun) in bed. You'll find flirting a cinch, orgasm easier, and discover new sexual territory to explore with your mate, even if the two of you have become fossilized on the edge of boredom. No matter where you stand sexually—innocent or uninhibited wanton —you will find information in this candid, explicit, and creative little book to make your love life steamier. Monogamy suddenly has a new cachet, not just out of fear of sexually transmitted disease, but from a longing for intimacy and connection. And vulnerable, sensation-bombarded humans need all the help we can get. (Please pay special attention to "Safe Sex with Strangers" on pages 168–172 for the most up-to-date information on sexually transmitted disease.)

I solemnly pledge that this book will help you a little, if it does not actually help you a lot. (Guaranteed by Loids of Long Island.)

What are my credentials? I'm an amateur in the true sense of that word, a lover. I love love. I love being in love. I love making love. And I've always been just a bit naughty. From Scarlett O'Hara and Amber St. Clare and Albert Ellis I gleaned early inspiration. I've always asked slightly embarrassing questions, and tried to hear and understand the answers. After a loving marriage and a fine postmarital blossoming, I want to share the insights I have collected, a few of my own, some from woman talk and pillow talk, much from the most respected experts.

Yes, the *Delicious Sex* regimen is tough. It has to be, because prudery and insecurity are like cellulite—blubber that is tough to melt away. But if you are faithful to the exercises, the payoffs will be a freer woman, liking yourself, being more lovable, a master of sensuality, a candidate for sexual bliss. There is no way you cannot emerge fitter, trimmer, prettier, wittier, more amusing, more relaxed, and healthier as well as sexually more confident and content. What can you lose? Only your self-doubt and that anxious uptight feeling.

GET READY TO START TODAY.

So what if it's Thursday or Saturday. Great sex is not like a diet. You don't have to start on Monday. Tonight is ideal. Just minutes a day are all you need. Set aside some time every day. No excuses. No headaches. No backaches. Nothing should come between you and the challenge of each chapter. Start by putting a lock on the bedroom door so no one can disturb you. And once you've moved to the exercises requiring a bedmate, don't let fatigue—real or imagined—sabotage you. Share a candy bar or a brandy or a porn film on your bedside videotape recorder and see if it doesn't wake up both of you enough to do an educational workout. Nothing is more refreshing than the sleep that follows great sex. (And don't be discouraged if it takes time to connect with that special man. Once you master pages 1 through 174, you'll be virtually irresistible.)

Even if you are ready for advanced sex techniques and exotica, start with the first chapter. Polish and refine your natural instincts and acquired skills.

Ecstasy beckons.

Go. Come.

Is This Book for You?

Long ago you achieved sexual confidence, and you almost always have great fun in bed. Is this book for you? Yes. As a skilled and gifted sexualist you will be curious to know what possible ecstasy still waits to be explored.

You suspect you don't really like sex . . . or, worse, the man you live with is less-than-noticeably lusty. Do you need this book? Yes. Unless it's a hormone deficiency, or serious psychopathology, it may not be too late to discover that sex can actually be fun. And funny.

You've been to bed with your college football star and his brother, your English professor, two legendary Casanovas, and the Entenmann's delivery man, and everyone says you're "very excellent." Do you need this book? Yes. Now that you're ready to focus on *quality.*

He's a darling—the high-school sweetheart you married twenty-five years ago—and you still make love 1.4 times a week, and passion is not what commitment is all about. Oh, sweetheart—this is the book for you.

Describe what you see in this inkblot. Be as relaxed and creative as you can.

1. If you saw Afghanistan being splintered by Russia surrounded by palm trees, score 10 points.
2. Are you seeing stilt walkers dancing with French-fried shrimp? Score 5 points.
3. Does it look like Brooke Shields eating a banana? Score 1 point.
4. It reminds you of the time you slipped carrying dinner to the table and fell face first into the spaghetti. Score 6 points.
5. It's definitely a graph of the gross national product of Peru. Score 9 points.
6. Two ballerinas are doing delicious things to Robert Redford. Score 0 points.

The Ink Blot Test

Take this Obsessional Rating Quiz, with or without your man. Check as many of the choices as apply.

I've never had sex that was as much fun as:

Watching "Miami Vice" _____
Pigging out on ice cream _____
Winning my company's incentive program _____
Cleaning my closets _____

Count 10 points for each check and add to the inkblot score. Under 10, buy this book. Over 20, you really need this book. If you score 35 or higher, steal this book if necessary.

Delicious
Sex

The Philosophy of Sexual Confidence

Y ou are about to embark on an adventure that can help you say good-bye forever to sexual anxiety and constricted ecstasy. The goal of the exercises in the *Delicious Sex* program is simple: sexual confidence. More than beauty, more than exotic lovemaking techniques, more than power or money, the secret of better sex is . . . sexual confidence—knowing as you start to make love even with a new partner that you will probably have a wonderful time and so will he. And if for some reason you don't . . . it's not your fault. No matter how sexually timid you are, no matter how sexually free, you are holding in your hand collected insights that will help you discover new sexual potential. At the same time, you will learn how to unleash the sexuality in the man you love and/or the man you play with.

Where does sexual confidence come from?

Beauty does not guarantee sexual confidence. A beautiful woman may walk into a crowded room knowing that she can attract the glance, if not the attention and perhaps the pursuit, of almost any man there. And it might seem that a great body, perfect breasts, endless legs, and a cover-girl face should guarantee that same confidence in bed. Sorry. Some of the world's great beauties are repressed, minimally orgasmic, or sensually deprived, wanting to be loved for their brains and not for their beauty, tormented by self-doubt and insecurity. Ask their lovers. Ask their analysts.

Sexual confidence comes from understanding your body and feeling comfortable inside it, knowing what turns you on and how to discover what pleases your man . . . knowing ultimately how to achieve your own sexual joy. That confidence comes with knowing that sex is not just vaginal intercourse, but hugging and kissing, caressing and stroking, mouths whispering, teasing, nibbling, sucking, every physical intimacy —and that the goal of sex is not orgasm but pleasure.

Indeed, some of the freest sexual spirits I know are far from great beauties. Not being able to compete in the Super Bowl of beauty, they may have cultivated their sexual expertise and ease as a way of getting the man and the intimacy they want. And along the way to sexual confidence, using sex to get what you want, to feel more desirable, to bolster your ego is not unusual. But one day you reach a higher level when sexy is not what you do but quite simply what you are. No artifice. No desperate motivations. No faking. It is really you.

We are all born sexy. Babies love playing with themselves. But sexual knowledge is learned, sexual expertise is collected, sexual confidence is acquired, and sexual tastes are developed over the years, just as tastes in art and music and poetry develop. It takes passionate enthusiasm. Still, in these times when casual sex is laced with peril and monogamy is embraced with renewed dedication, keeping sex hot is a challenge. I believe it's a challenge worth Mount Everests of effort.

This is a book about feeling good in bed. It's about great sex. For many women sex is never more exhilarating as when they're with someone they love. For others the hottest moment is the first time, the instant before a single zipper unzips. This is not a book about love. It's about making love . . . making all the reality steamier.

The good news about sex is that it never runs out. The earlier you start, the longer it lasts. The better it is, the more you want. As Julia Child says, "Bon appétit."

Feeling Good in Your Skin

Sexual feeling comes from within. The brain is always in charge. And it's hard to feel good about yourself—impossible to feel irresistibly sexy—if you can't stand how you look. Go ahead. List your flaws. Flabby thighs. Breasts too small or too big. Blubbery knees. Freckles in all the wrong places. Pop-out tummy or pear-shaped bottom. Or no bottom at all, and hips like a young boy's. Is there any woman who is content with her body, who wouldn't change something if a genie gave her three wishes—away with the stretch marks, the crow's feet, the pudginess? Even Jane Fonda and Raquel Welch weren't happy with the state of their anatomy. That's why Jane perfected her strenuous workouts and why women everywhere have signed up to share the burn. That's why Raquel does all the dutiful, healthy routines and yoga she advocates. They both make forty look better than twenty-five.

Do whatever you can to reorganize or rehabilitate your less-than-perfect face and body. Exercise? Absolutely. Stretch and strengthen. Work out every day if you can. Walk a few miles, and dance like a fool. And there's nothing wrong with plastic surgery, either, if you really need it and your expectations are realistic.

But moaning and groaning over real and imagined imperfections that cannot be corrected or that you will not work on is silly and counter-sexy. Sexual confidence means finding the way to be comfortable in your existing body, no matter how imperfect, how used, how (excuse my explicit language) aged. A heart-shaped derrière, twice as much thigh as *Vogue* would permit . . . stop brooding about it. The wonderful truth is there are men who will love you as you are and men who will love you because you are the way you are. So you aren't the face or the body Eileen Ford is looking for. Do you know that there are men's magazines devoted to women with 38DD breasts and cheesecake featuring chubby pinups? Tastes do vary. Voluptuous or scrawny, you are somebody's potential sex object. (And being a sex object is *good* in a book about sex. This is not a guide to being a bank president. For all I know, you *are* a bank president.)

Ideally you might prefer to lose the ten pounds that keep you from classical perfection or the twenty pounds that keep you from chic. Till then, forget about it. Forget about the cellulite. Or that your nipples go in or out or whatever it is you think they shouldn't do. Never apologize. Never call attention to the flaws that torment you. Your liking your body will help him love it more. And as you blossom sexually, he's going to be so excited by your amazing responsiveness, he will be oblivious to the specifics that you might obsess about. Stop.

Yes, do get in shape. Ten extra pounds will be infinitely more attractive if they're toned solid by exercise. Exercise will also give you energy, agility, and improved posture. Serious aerobics and advanced workouts not only lengthen muscles and trim inches but also help you be more versatile in bed. And more graceful. And more capable of putting yourself into the position that makes you hot. He won't have to throw you around or tug you into place when you are strong and flexible. You stretch and bounce and can meet him stroke for stroke. And you thought those pelvic tilts in aerobics class were just designed to firm your backside.

And don't get anxious if your private parts don't look precisely like the rose-petaled labia you see in *Penthouse* centerfolds. Look again. Each woman's vulva is different. Artists have celebrated the variations of vulva in painting and sculpture. In her book *Liberating Masturbation,* Betty Dodson includes her drawings of women from this perspective. Studying her pictures and looking at yourself in a mirror, you'll see . . . you're just another mysteriously wonderful vulva.

If you really look much better dressed than undressed, treat yourself to exquisite underwear and beautiful nightgowns that give you the bo-som lift you want and conceal what begs to be hidden. A bedroom designed to flatter you helps, too. Creams, body smoothers, pedicures, facials, all-over body silking with a loofah or salt and almond oil can't help but make you feel sexier. Of course you smell sweet, because you bathe and wash, and you know that the vagina is self-cleaning and douching can be a neurotic obsession—your clean natural musk is highly erotic. A week in a spa that combines frenzied exercise with every imaginable beauty treatment is exactly what any woman would love to launch, even a modest rehab—but if the tab for all that profes-sional pampering is too high, you can match most of it at home with the help of a beauty book that gives recipes for yogurt and cucumber facials, milk baths, olive-oil hair conditioners, mayonnaise hand care, and cream, cream, cream.

There's something to be said for going-to-bed makeup, too. That can mean creaming evening makeup away and painting a new face—flushed and dewy. Perhaps a dab of rosy blusher here and there on your body, too. A man friend of mine, much pursued by women, marveled once about the woman then in his life, who wore little or no makeup all day but did a complete theatrical paint job for bedtime. He loved it, and was touched by her efforts to play into his fantasies by constantly changing her image.

If you've done everything to enhance the anatomy you've got, or vowed to get in the days ahead, or have absorbed the message of this chapter, you are ready to relax and feel good in your skin. Here comes the morning sun. *He* opens his eyes. Nothing can chase that sensual glow. The body he sees is the body that gave him so much pleasure last night, the woman who responded with an intensity that never ceases to astonish and please him. That's your body, you. Of course, your sexiest negligee is draped not far away, so you can slip into it and get breakfast. Unless he insists on getting it for you.

Dress for Sexcess

What's hot and what's not in furs, shoes, handbags, gloves, play clothes, coats, jewelry? Certain items of clothing are sexual clichés. Black stockings with seams, a lacy garter belt, spike heels and ankle straps that wind or tie, lace-edged teddies, and nightgowns slit to here and there are erotic icons. And certain garb is so downright dowdy, even the untrained sensibility knows instinctively that it is anti-erotic. The polyester muu-muu, flannel granny gowns, panty girdles, hiking shoes, Peter Pan collars. Clearly, zippers that gap and safety-pinned anything convey a message not likely to fuel passion.

I wish I could say beauty doesn't count. But it does. Still, there are wonderful faces that are cold as porcelain and beautiful bodies hidden in very serious dresses (great for the office or lunch with your accountant, but no erotic allure), and unmatching ragbag separates so tacky you shouldn't be caught dead in them at the Laundromat. Blatant flash isn't necessarily hot. A draped lamé dress with half the bodice missing may stop traffic, but it's not nearly as sexy as a healthy unfettered body moving with subtle animal allure in cover-up bias-cut red silk. Attitude is powerful. An unfashionably plump woman in a flattering tunic and fringe, moving as if she *knows* she is sexy, *is* sexy.

There is a tantalizing perversity in dressing for sexcess. One man's

turn-on is another man's ho-hum. What is sexy on you may not be sexy at all on your best friend. Almost anything will seem sexier on a really sexual woman, and nothing will elevate the thermal pow of a determinedly uptight creature. So experiment with what's classically sexy— what makes you look good and feel hot. Then refine your style once you get a sense of his special fantasies.

Vaguely sheer can be hotter than totally see-through, and full sleeves slit from shoulder to wrist that occasionally fall open can be more erotic than show-all cleavage. Play up your best features. Slits to here are great if the flash of flesh they reveal is great. Fringe is hot—silk fringe, suede fringe—as is leather . . . leather when it really fits. Going against your type can be very exciting if it isn't silly—a touch of sleaze on a very elegant woman, little-girl rompers on a statuesque grownup, siren-black satin gloves and dominatrix underwear on a perky gamine.

Soft fabrics are sexier than stiff. Fabrics that cling to bodies where cling flatters—silk jersey, thin and soft as a baby's skin, and tissue wool crepe—are hot. Lace can be teasing. Nubby tweeds, stern blue serge, cheap sateen, and iridescent rayon sleaze are not. Velvet is sexy.

Red is hot. Orange is not. Baby blue is sexier than yellow. Black is sexy, but black isn't everything. White can be sexier than black. The colors you look best in make you glow.

Furs that wrap are hot. And fuzzy little furs. Curly white lamb. Fur ear muffs are hot. Nanook of the North is not. Mink you are lost inside and striped skins miss the point. Animal heads are antierotic. Flying foxtails are hot. Mink with you naked inside is a kick.

Tight jeans on tight derrières are hot, and short shorts that accidentally reveal just a hint of rounded bottom. Crinkly cotton balloon pants slit from ankle to mid-thigh are a lovely tease. Huge sweaters with a deep V over narrow mini-skirts are hot, and cut-off T-shirts that reveal a perfect midriff; also, bikinis and bathing suits that bare and frame your most appealing features. A ruffled pinafore with nothing underneath can be hot. Not: Bermuda shorts, big shirts, baggy pants, too-short cutoffs. Most neckties. Army-issue anything. Too-tight cardigans. Cable stitch anywhere. Nubby knits. Chartreuse, taupe, leaf green. Militant-message T-shirts.

Chiffon evening pajamas that show a silhouette when the light's behind you are properly provocative. Black satin with bare breasts moving inside, sweetheart necklines, empire gowns, ruffled sheers, slits revealing glorious legs, and lace-up merry widows are hot. Peplums can be sexy, and dresses that shimmer, seeming to reveal more than they conceal. Ditto a well-cut tuxedo made just for you, with a black lace bustier instead of a dress shirt. Real gardenias in your hair are hot. Wilted, they are not. Tents, shifts, most flowered prints, most shirtwaists, and linebacker shoulder pads are antierotic.

Jewelry that sparkles is hot: diamonds on bare white skin, and antique marcasite. Nothing is more erotic than a long single strand of pearls falling between naked breasts barely revealed by a silk satin blouse. Thin gold chains in odd places, around an ankle or a slender waist. A long gold chain with a locket that swings when you dance and taps your mons veneris when you walk. Serious chains that intimate bondage, even handcuffs, are a special fetish.

Sexy coats drape and have rich fox collars that frame your throat. White cashmere trenchcoats are hot, also velvet and satin capes. Fringed silk and cut-velvet shawls are great over bare shoulders in icy air conditioning and over bare everything at home. Fake fur is rarely hot. Ditto big coats.

Snake handbags are hot. So are soft little pouches that let out a whiff of your perfume when you open them, and trim attaché cases that reveal a sexy nightgown, a split of champagne, a toothbrush, and your clear intention of spending the night. Not hot: huge bags overflowing with the effluvia of your disordered life. Canvas sacks that slam into him when you walk down the street. Serious handbags. Purses that resemble animals or fish or giant Life Saver candies. (Cute is usually not hot.)

A sexy hat is a little doodad with a spiderweb veil that does incredible things to your incredible eyes. A newsboy cap with yards of silken hair tucked inside can be hot. A Stetson on the right face is magical. So is a big fur hat that drips into your sooty eyelashes. Not sexy: serious hats, a babushka over curlers, most turbans. A nurse's cap or a velvet riding hat might satisfy certain fetishists.

Very high heels are still the sexiest. And slim suede or soft leather boots that go over the knees (especially in bed). Straps that tie up the leg can be hot. And graceful red shoes. Expensive handmade pumps that make your foot look spectacular. Riding boots. Very-high-heeled boots. Boots with fringe. Suede boots that crush down softly. Fur-trimmed boots and red snake anything. Not hot: nurse's shoes, dirty sneakers, fashionably ugly shoes, oxfords, Cuban heels, storm-trooper boots, orange-and-gold tapestry ballerina slippers. Special effects that can be hot: heels so high you can barely walk, shoes to wear only in bed, mirrored heels so he can see himself as he licks your ankle.

Long, slinky pull-on gloves in satin or the softest kid with little pearl buttons at the wrist are hot. Beautiful gloves are always hot, hottest in black, red, and white. Never hot in forest green. Knit gloves with different-colored fingers are cute, not hot. Also not: cheap gloves, fake leather, rubber dishwashing gloves, hot-pad mitts.

Very hot: take him shopping if he wants to come along . . . especially where you can act out your fantasy of making love in the fitting room.

Of course, sexual feelings come from within and are not created by the wisp or whoosh or flash of what you wear. But knowing what makes you irresistible and what arouses him—feeling good in your clothes, at home in your skin—can't help but make you like yourself more and feel infinitely sexier.

INTIMATIONS OF UNDERWEAR

Your job may require you to dress in impeccable gabardine and flannel, even to wear a crisp and efficient uniform, but what you wear underneath tells the story. Underneath is the real you. Or the you that you long to be. Underwear is a safe and inexpensive outlet for sexual fantasy.

Imagine a tall, tough-talking punk-haired brunette stepping out of her corduroy jeans and ripping off a denim workshirt to reveal a rust silk chemise and bikini panties etched in black lace, with nothing under it but a perfect body. What an exquisitely erotic shock.

Garter belts. Ultra-sheer stockings. Wisps of black chiffon with heart-shaped cutouts. Bikinis with a bunny fur tail. (Oh, why not!) How about a luxurious taffeta merry widow, perhaps just for walking around the house, a white cotton chemise with little pink rosebuds embroidered on it, or even a nailhead-studded leather bikini . . . something really trashy, with cutouts for nipples? If you've got great legs, collect stockings, garters, and spike-heel shoes. Wispy lace half-bras and see-through teddies frame perfect breasts. And ruffly silk garments with seams in the right places mask flaws and lift droops.

Yes, I know. You are the attendance counselor at P.S. 5. A medical librarian. The Cardinal's secretary. A teller at Chase Manhattan Bank. Dress accordingly, but pick your underwear to make you feel sexy all day long.

Let the silk caress your skin. Feel your breasts moving inside your barely there bra. Smile at the secret of your sleazy garter belt or your tiger-striped body suit. And wiggle and preen knowing that your prettiest scarlet silk panties don't conceal your strawberry tattoo . . . it's not permanent, of course. No wonder you seem sexier. You are.

Encourage your man to discard his baggy elasticized boxer shorts and those utilitarian Jockeys with the rotting elastic. Happily, as men get into body-building and rehab, they discover French bikinis in black and bright colors, and a really uninhibited man might even discover *your* silk bikinis. (There's a fantasy to explore.) Of course, men are only just beginning to experience the joy of being sex objects. Now that women have proven that we aren't only sex objects (as if we ever were), we can enjoy the gratification inherent in all the wild and beautiful paraphernalia of dressing up underneath.

Even if you buy all your underwear in a local department store, be sure to send for a collection of mail-order underwear catalogues. The Victoria's Secret mail-order brochure is yours just for calling (800) 821-0001. The Evelyn Rainbird catalogue of lingerie, leatherwear, and sex toys costs $3, and "Lady Annabelle Sensual Lingerie for the Rubenesque Woman" is $2 (refunded with the first order); write Evelyn Rainbird, Department 006L, P.O. Box 6500, Englewood, NJ 07631. Voyages' catalogue (try their feather bra and bikini) is $3.50 from Voyages, 330 Townsend Street, Suite 16, San Francisco, CA 94107. A few years ago Bloomingdale's mailed out an astonishing lingerie booklet that has become a collector's classic for underwear fetishists.

Ask your man to help you choose a lingerie wardrobe. Go through the catalogues together. Even if you never order a thing, you may find yourselves sharing fantasies that really make the evening sizzle.

NIGHTCLOTHES

Some people think sleeping nude is sexy. But nothing is sexier than a sheer black nightgown edged with peekaboo lace lying in a pouf on the floor beside the bed the morning after. Nightclothes are theater. Night-

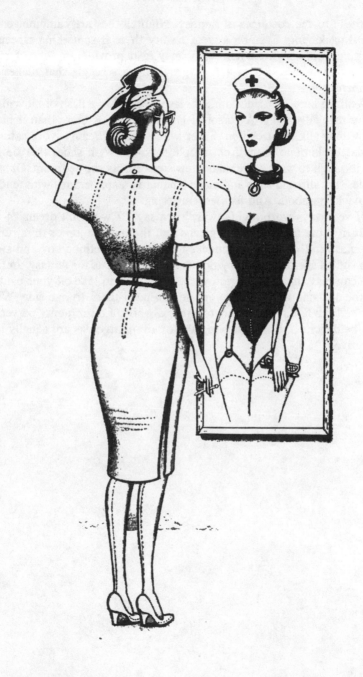

clothes are the costumes of fantasy. Nightclothes are camouflage and artful packaging. Even on a great beauty there is something especially exciting about nightclothes. They may also provide an aura of resistance that invites conquest . . . providing a struggle that makes the moment hotter.

A slit to here. The sides of the breast revealed in a flash of movement. A tie that falls away. A gusset of lace that reveals more than it hides. Baby blue silk. Red chiffon. Sheer white voile. Creamy ivory satin. A fur-edged kimono. Lace from nipple to knee. With shoes that tie and are too high to walk more than a few steps across the bedroom. Or satin mules that slip and slide and make a naughty slap, perhaps with tendrils of black marabou. And feathers fluttering.

"I've always worn nightgowns," you say. "I wouldn't dream of—"

Burn those flannel granny gowns and the opaque junior miss ruffled pajamas, that pink cotton smocked number. Something coy and sweet in a ruffled see-through baby doll is fine, even a cue for fantasy. In fact, you can play the virgin, if you wish, and refuse to take off your panties. In the struggle to persuade you, he can push them to one side. When you've been living and loving together a while, a bit of pouty perversity can be delicious. Primly flowing Victorian nightgowns are equally provocative.

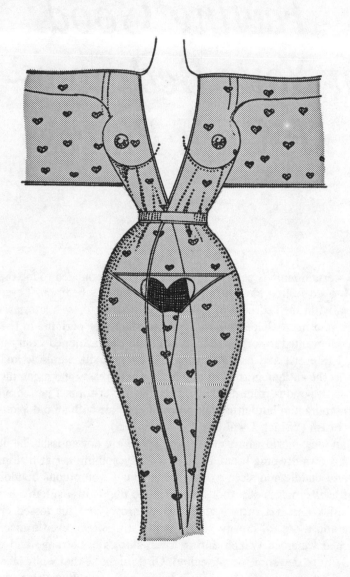

Feeling Good in Your Bedroom— Private Places

A certain famous wildly rich Don Juan once confided to me that he loved feeling like an intruder in a woman's bedroom—even, or especially, in the bedroom of his wife. He wanted to see Victorian lace, ruffles, and heart-shaped pillows . . . to smell her perfume in the bed linen. He wanted to surprise her sitting at an old-fashioned vanity table, draped in eyelet and lace, admiring herself in a silk camisole and tap pants in the antique mirror, or powdering her breasts and creaming her arms with potions from dozens of precious silver-topped jars, pretending to ignore him but letting him smooth her hair with an old Victorian silver brush ("which I will buy," he promised).

In an ideal world where money and space are not an issue, he might have his own dressing room, bath, and study, joining her at bedtime to play and cuddle and sleep in her outrageously voluptuous boudoir. It might evoke images of a thousand and one nights in a sultan's harem, with thick Oriental carpets and paisley throws and fur tossed everywhere and a nest of downy pillows and satin sheets, even a nice old-fashioned waterbed (which during lovemaking does strange and wonderful things that some people enjoy). Or it might be that white lace and cotton Victorian retreat, or a plush velvet and satin movie-star setting. Since money doesn't matter, there will be a Roman bath, perhaps just behind a screen, with Jacuzzi and sauna and heated towels and a small fridge filled with splits of champagne, fresh squeezed orange juice, raspberries whenever in season, and chocolate truffles.

For those of us who are not yet as rich as Croesus, here are some wise investments:

1. Down pillows and quilts.
2. Supercale sheets that get softer with each washing.
3. Mirrors where you want them and Mylar on the ceiling.
4. Lights that dim and fabric throws to shade a lamp in colors that flatter.
5. Pink bulbs.
6. Candles, scented and plain. Potpourri.
7. Beautiful fruit in a bowl by the bed.
8. A sturdy stand-up tray for supper and breakfast in bed.
9. A great mattress.
10. Window shades or curtains that keep out the light.
11. Rubber furniture cups to keep the bed from moving on a bare floor.
12. A small trunk or basket by your bed for sex toys, massage oil, and erotica.
13. A big trunk to tuck away anything that looks messy and serious.
14. A lock on the door.
15. Cork or velvet or other soundproofing if you need aural privacy. Music can act as a sound barrier, too.
16. Fresh flowers and a cut-glass box of chocolate truffles.
17. A canopy of filmy curtains, and, if you don't have a fourposter or a headboard, perhaps handles on the wall to hold on to in moments of uncontrollable ecstasy (or to keep from sliding off your satin sheets).

Some people think that a television set in the bedroom is a sure sign that romance has faded. For someone like me, who truly nests in bed, it's hard to imagine the TV anywhere else. I can't think of anything cosier or more intimate than sharing a pint of caramel swirl ice cream and watching a great old movie together. And then there is your VCR, ready to indulge an appetite for dirty movies.

Even if you aren't sharing your life with a man, you need these luxuries (especially the chocolate truffles, which are a chemical balm for heartbreak). If the budget is lean and space at a premium, haunt yard sales and improvise a vanity from someone's cast-off wicker side table and a fabulous mirror you frame with eyelet ruffles. Give yourself the most sensuous nest you can devise, and magical lighting. Consider a Murphy bed tucked into a mirrored closet, or whether a small balcony might enhance romance. Send the kids on a sleepaway, bribe your roommate to camp out with a friend. Pamper yourself with perfume and lotions and fresh yellow freesias, and luxuriate in bed as if you were an heiress.

Body Language

Your body speaks for you whether you are aware of it or not. Your arms clasped across your chest signal defensiveness. Palm and wrist exposed is a subliminal message of openness. You touch your throat or your breast or steady his hand as he lights your cigarette (the only thing I miss having quit smoking). That touch says "I'm interested." Alas, here's an area where men and women are not created equal. A man can signal his sexual intentions blatantly—standing with his legs apart, his thumb in his belt, index finger pointed toward his crotch, catching your glance and trying to hold it. Without a word uttered, you get his message: "I'm hot. I'm a man. I'm ready. I want you." Unfortunately, the sexually aggressive male and even the New Man may find it difficult to cope with too-direct an approach from a woman. Though some men are excited and respond to the body language of a woman who seems definitely interested (and will read disinterest if some encouragement is missing), we have to be more subtle.

An open relaxed stance signals receptivity. You can stroke your arm, touch your breast, almost accidentally press your breast against his arm when he takes yours to cross the street, hold his glance just a beat too long. Smile. Giggle. Tossing your hair is great. Playing with the stem of your wineglass. Leaning forward. Pressing your thigh against his. Putting your head to one side. This is old-fashioned flirting, an art long overdue for revival. These gestures—a lot of them you make unconsciously—suggest your interest. In him. And in sex. If you know you're inclined to be stiff, repressed, closed off, it will take a conscious effort to relax and send out positive signals. Don't let your body say no when your head or your heart or your libido says yes.

BODY LANGUAGE AT HOME

It's easy to get bogged down in domestic trivia at home . . . to shut off your sexual antennae with the man you love, the man you have been sleeping with for a while. All your unconscious moves and facial expressions say your mind is elsewhere, your emotions are distracted. It may take a calculated effort to change the message, to convey your interest in sex, to remind him how hot you can be and rekindle his fire.

A quick glance through *Playboy* and *Penthouse* will give you a crash course in body talk. See what the Pets and the Playmates are up to. It's not only what they're wearing or not wearing, although whimsical semidress can be wonderfully sexy—it's what they're doing with their fingers, their legs, the inviting arrangements of lush rumps and open legs, spike-heels, ankle straps swinging, ropes of pearls dangling, eyes and mouths speaking more clearly than any words.

If your usual at-home garb is cutoffs and a T-shirt or a little plissé pastel morning coat, you won't want to suddenly swoop down on an unwary mate wearing ostrich plumes and thigh-high pirate boots just because you saw it in a men's magazine. I'm only suggesting that certain arrangements of your anatomy in bed or tucked into an easy chair can be highly provocative. Understanding male fantasy can get you . . . anywhere.

Here's a doll they call Sugar Baby. Not that much makeup but enough, hair fluffed, abbreviated satin teddy exposing one breast, one leg crossed high over the other, spotlighting painted toes and graceful arches in sexy satin mules. It's a fine position in which to knit or watch television or read a book or even write one—and what an invitation. And look at Veronique. One long black satin glove on, the other off, a wisp of black ruffles falling off her tanned torso. She lies face down on the pillow, her eyes looking back at him, one leg pulled up, her derrière arched an inch or two off the bed. No mistaking what she's got on her mind.

Half dress is so hot. A wisp of silk shawl with fringe just brushing your clitoris. White stockings and Mary Jane shoes and nothing else. A beaded vest and skin. Know that he loves to be the voyeur. That he's watching you at your dressing table, half naked, studying your image . . . only partially concealed behind the screen, bending over to buckle the strap of your shoe, languorously pulling stockings on and off. I suppose with some men you may have to drape yourself over the TV set to get a glance, but it's worth some extra perfume.

Are you resisting this as phony, contrived, sexist, and neurotic? Why would you give less thought to your sex life than you do to your career or your home? You wouldn't hand in a résumé to a prospective employer written in pencil, or expect to impress dinner guests with Hostess Twinkies à la mode.

Body language is the nonverbal message that lets you say what you really mean: I love my body. I love sex. I love to make love. I want to make love to you.

How to Eat a Fig—The Sensuous Woman

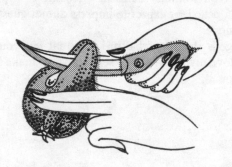

For some, sex is a rather simple act of penetration and friction leading to orgasm. For others the goal is power, security, money, or an affirmation of one's appeal. Often it is an act of intimacy and a way to communicate love. For any one of us it can also be pleasure . . . extraordinary sensual pleasure.

Some sensualists are born, I suppose. They walk around high on beauty, rapturously smelling flowers, swooning over sunsets, lyricizing over fresh cut grass, sniffing perfume and finding the scent of raspberries in your wine, weeping over Chopin, calling your attention to the sound of the mounted policeman's horse's hoofbeats on the street. But most of us need sensory stimulation. We are too busy, too intellectually oriented to notice the feel of things even as we hold them or appreciate the subtle scents that fill the air. We see a rose and never dream of stopping to see how it smells. We lie in bed and kiss, never becoming transfixed by skin—how it smells, in the sun, after hard work, the just-bathed soapy smell, how it feels inside where it is smooth, here where it is rough and hairy, the steel of muscle, the jut of bone, the feel against your cheek, your tongue, your lips, your fingertip, warmth against your own warmth, weight as it presses against you.

In most of us the visual sense is reasonably developed. We use our eyes (before our ears and brains) to make our earliest romantic decisions, but even eyes miss out in bed if they are always closed in modesty or ecstasy. The nose is timid, the ears shut down, and the mouth is sometimes so busy it hasn't a chance to savor.

Let's Earn a Ph.D. in Sensuality by Learning to Eat a Fig

1.   Buy a fresh fig—it doesn't matter if the skin is green or black. Study the skin, its folds and markings. (Since fresh figs are rare, I hope you won't put off having delicious sex while waiting for the figs to arrive.)

2.   Cut a cross in the stem end of the fig. (This cross has no religious significance, but if it spooks you too much to cut a cross, by all means cut a star. A crescent probably won't work, nor will a hammer and sickle.)

3.   Squeeze the fig with four fingers till it opens like the petals of a flower.

4.   Study the astonishing contrast between the unthrilling skin and the amazing blush and varying pinks of the flesh.

5.   Smell the fig. It's a subtle scent but uniquely figgy. Smell it again.

6.   Lick the fig. The taste is subtle too, wonderfully organic. Lick it again.

7.   Rub your mouth and chin with the fig. How do you feel about the wetness? Lick your fingers. It's fun to be piggy.

8.   Bite the fig and swallow it. Take another bite and taste it as it rests on your tongue. Taste the sweetness and the tart undertone. Feel the texture of the fig—it's not at all like pizza, is it, or like a lamb chop? It's a fig. Savor its unique figginess.

You have now had the total sensual experience of a fig. Try these sensory exercises:

1. Walk into a bakery where they are actually baking bread.
2. Rub cocoa butter into your skin.
3. Grind some coffee beans and savor the smell.
4. Treat yourself to brand-new laundered and ironed cotton sheets.
5. Bury your face in a peony.
6. Rub your lips with the fresh-cut edge of a jalapeño pepper.
7. Press an ice-cold glass against your mouth.
8. Go into a wonderful apothecary or bath shop and sniff all the perfumed soaps to find the ones you like.
9. Rub a sprig of fresh rosemary on your wrist.
10. Smell your skin after you've been in the sun.
11. Walk into a pickle store and inhale deeply.
12. Pour some poire or framboise into a glass—sniff it—put some on the edge of your tongue.
13. Look at your lover's face upside down.
14. Lick the skin of a washed orange.
15. Make love in total darkness. Touch when you don't know where your fingers are landing; slide from smooth to stubbly to soft, to the wetness of his mouth. Do it to yourself, also in the dark.
16. Make love outdoors in daylight. Smell the grass and mud. Smell your own smells. Watch the clouds.
17. Lick his elbow. Lick his knee.
18. Delight in how smooth he feels when you've dusted him all over with baby powder.
19. Smell his after-lovemaking sweat. Blow on it.
20. Lift your breast and feel the heft of it in your hand.
21. Find the softest skin on your own body.
22. Play with the springy hairs, yours and his.

A Dozen Wonderful Things to Do with Your Mouth

1. Suck a passionfruit.
2. Peel a grape with your teeth and eat it.
3. Taste the difference when it's homemade mayonnaise.
4. Suck his fingers.
5. Suck his fingers after he plays with you.
6. Try bacon and peanut butter on a banana.
7. Let chocolate melt on your tongue.

8. Swirl a great wine in your glass, smell it, and sip it, holding a bit in the back of your mouth and hissing the air in.
9. Pop red caviar eggs with your tongue.
10. Buy a bag of fresh lichees and eat them very slowly.
11. Chew licorice, savor its unique taste, and study your mouth tinted black.
12. Pick blackberries from a bush and make them into a pie, and share it with people you love.

What Is
a Great Lover?

He speaks:

She loves to make love. She concentrates . . . on me . . . on
where we are. I feel her there. She can be aggressive. She can be
passive, provocatively passive at times. She can be wild and animal,
tender and loving. Sometimes I catch her looking at me and I
know, yes, it's sex and lust and heat, but I also know it's the two of
us. She is full of compliments and makes the most wonderful
sounds. I always know what's pleasing her. Sometimes she is
turned on before I come near her, but her capacity and desire to
make love never come across as a petulant demand. She doesn't
sulk or act rejected or make me feel guilty if I'm exhausted or too
distracted to make love. And she is sensitive and very loving with
me when she's not in the mood. She has an amazing ability to let
go, to expose herself, her needs. I love to watch her lose herself in
sexual feeling. She has orgasms easily, sometimes so powerful,
sometimes so many, she makes me feel like Superman. She can be
cute and silly and funny and make me laugh in bed and then drive
me crazy with her ferocity. She is basically willing to try anything,
at least once. Her fantasies are hot, and I love acting them out with

her. She can do that too, surprising me at unexpected moments by walking into my office naked in her raincoat or wrapping my birthday gift in a centerfold from *Penthouse.*

She speaks:

He is a scholar of women. He really likes women, but I always feel he is focused on me. I feel he is really here . . . with me, my body, my mouth, his pleasure . . . is me. I feel wonderfully secure with him. I don't have to hide anything. I can be as wild and kinky, as loving, as vulnerable, as crazed as I want to be. He is extraordinarily sensual, in love with skin and flesh, sensitive to smells . . . he makes me feel I am nectar and ambrosia. His hands are everywhere, wonderfully knowing and full of surprises. He takes me to a sexual level I've never reached before. With his lips, tongue, teeth—with his breath—he elicits responses that amaze me. And nothing makes him hotter than the intensity of my response. Often he is willing to put himself into a sexual mood (when he's not really there), and he has no trouble playing into my fantasies or leading me into his. He loves intimacy, is not afraid to let go, to expose his vulnerability, to be totally passive. He is the best kisser. He loves to hug. He is an incurable cuddler. He is fun and funny, playful, inventive, curious. He cries. Sometimes from sad memories or silly regrets, sometimes from joy. He is romantic and thoughtful and needs me.

Mapping the Female Erogenous Zones

Your brain is your body's most powerful erogenous zone, obviously. It can be bossy, hopelessly opinionated and perverse. (Everything you'll read in this book is designed to liberate it from bigotry and countererotic impulses.) Understanding your own anatomy is just the beginning.

Ears. Blowing and very wet tongues are highly overrated, but a subtle teasing with lips, gentle teeth, and just the tip of the tongue can add to arousal.

Eyelids. Yes. Also, eyelashes kissing the cheekbones are hot.

Fingers and toes. Vulnerable to licking and sucking, but not quite the electricity felt by many men.

Inside elbows, wrists, and knees. Vulnerable to kisses, licks, and the fantasy that suddenly your lover has discovered a secret orifice.

Palms. Yes. Especially wet kisses.

Under arms, along the pectoral muscle. Sometimes susceptible to pressure, firm stroking, and gentle nibbles.

Skin. Feathery touches everywhere . . . stroking, tracing your body as if he were drawing you with his finger . . . can set off tremors of excitement. At the right moment, with the right man, some women will be ignitable from head to toe.

Derrière and inner thighs. Alternating firm and gentle stroking in rhythmic circles and squeezing can be an instant turn-on. Teasing touches of the thighs and seemingly accidental brushing of the vulva can create an electric charge.

Vaginal lips and surrounding territory. A concentration of nerve endings makes this a hot spot.

Mons veneris. Firm pressure of the palm can be intensely exciting, especially when the thumb just brushes the clitoris.

Anus. Pressure alone can be exciting for some, penetration the ultimate thrill for others.

Neck. The erotic spark is electrical for both men and women.

Mouth. Kissing, biting, probing . . . making love to him with your mouth . . . can be highly erotic.

Nipples and breasts. Touching, licking, nibbling, sucking, kissing, squeezing . . . more or less, what's hottest depends on the woman. Some women can climax from nipple play alone.

The G-spot. An especially sensitive area in the anterior wall of the vagina that responds to hard thrusting and pressure. Sexologists argue, but women who have it don't need to be convinced. (See pages 74–76.)

Clitoris. Yes, it's tiny and shy (retreating when it gets really hot), but the clitoris (plural: clitorides) has only one purpose in life—pleasure. A hood, a glans, and a shaft mostly hidden by the inner vaginal lips (the labia minora), the clitoris nestles on the front end of the vulva, below the mons veneris. Its myriad nerve endings make it the most sensitive spot in your body (and some have more nerve endings than others). With arousal, the shaft swells and blood rushes in, bringing a glow of pleasure to the whole pelvic area.

An Exercise Primer for the Kegel Workout

Aplayful friend once assured me that every woman has a Kegel muscle, named after the daring Dr. Kegel, a gynecologist who almost lost a finger examining the vaginal tract of a patient with a highly developed flex. It didn't start out quite so sexy, actually. Dr. Arthur Kegel came up with the idea of contracting and then relaxing the pubococcygeal muscle as a way to control urinary incontinence.

That's the muscle you can squeeze to give yourself an orgasm (well, some women can, and do) . . . the muscle you can flex to hold in water when you douche . . . the muscle you contract to give an extra squeeze or two to his penis when he comes. Indeed, studies show that the strength of this pelvic muscle can affect orgasmic response.

First you have to find the muscle, of course. Put your finger inside your vagina and squeeze. That's it. Still not sure? There are gadgets to help you, and detailed information in Lonnie Barbach's *For Yourself* and *The G-Spot* by Ladas, Whipple, and Perry.

No need now for leotard, leg warmers, exercise mat, or disco music. You can squeeze and flex the Kegel way—three-second flex, three-second relax, ten times—anytime, anywhere. You can squeeze and flex at your desk, at the library, at the drafting board, while driving your car, in the bathtub. Eventually you might do 100 ten-second contractions a day—Olympic-contender level.

Everyone responds to a warm, friendly hug. His penis will too when your toned pubococcygeal learns to contract at your command. Quick, affectionate squeezes timed with his orgasm can produce ecstasy. And a better-toned pelvis will make you happier, too.

You Are Your Own Best Friend— Masturbation

Do you love yourself enough? How do you really feel about masturbation? Take this quiz. Check the answers that sound like your own.

I Do Not/Rarely/Often/Compulsively Masturbate Because

a. It's impossible for a sculptor to work with hair on her hands.
b. I get more sex than I can handle already.
c. I'm waiting for the man in my dreams to show me how.
d. My mommy will be angry if I touch myself down there.
e. I don't want to spend my life in the loony bin for a few hot thrills.
f. I'm an upstanding, law-abiding citizen.
g. When my love life is great and I have sex often, it makes me hungry for more.
h. I do it better than anyone else.
i. I'm nearsighted already. I don't want to go blind.
j. I hate having such a good time all by myself.
k. I hate having a good time.

The experts respond:
a, e, i. If you'd listened to Dr. Ruth and everyone else writing about

sex for the past twenty years, you'd know by now that there's no way masturbation causes blindness, hairy palms, or mental illness.

b. Good for you. More sex than you desire can only be slightly less pleasing than all the sex you might want. You might be interested to know that men and women who rate their sexual relationships as "satisfying" masturbate too.

c. A good lover can teach you much that you don't know about your body. But why wait? Finding your own pleasure buttons can make you happy now alone, and happy later as a more responsive lover. If you're puzzled, confused, embarrassed, and not yet liberated enough—even after reading this far—buy Lonnie Barbach's book *For Yourself.*

d. Really? How old are you anyway? Twenty-three, twenty-nine, forty-two . . . do you still use your Water-Pik every day and drink three glasses of milk and take off your galoshes in the movies as Mommy told you to? Mom probably masturbates herself.

f. Masturbation is not against the law in any of the fifty states or the District of Columbia.

g. No wonder you masturbate often . . . I wouldn't call it "compulsive." In the words of the *Delicious Sex* motto: "Too much of a good thing is never enough."

h. Bravo. And no reason why you can't use your knowledge to show him what pleases you.

j. It's true, good times are even better shared. Masturbating with a friend is twice as much fun. Still, when you think how silly it is to tango alone, you have to be grateful that masturbation does not require a partner.

k. You win. Masturbation feels good. You wouldn't want that. It's a little like giving yourself a trip to France or a fur coat. Only it's free. Be miserable if that's what makes you happy.

There are women who masturbate freely, happily—often; with or without a mate beside them, with or without a satisfying level of lovemaking in their lives. "I can't remember when I first discovered how wonderful this feels," a woman friend confides. Yet there are women who never touch themselves—in secret, unspoken of but often—without a faint touch of embarrassment or guilt. There are women who play with themselves only in periods when an erotic playmate is lacking. And, at the farthest reaches of erotic deprivation, there are women who do not or cannot masturbate and rarely or never experience orgasm, either with a lover or on their own.

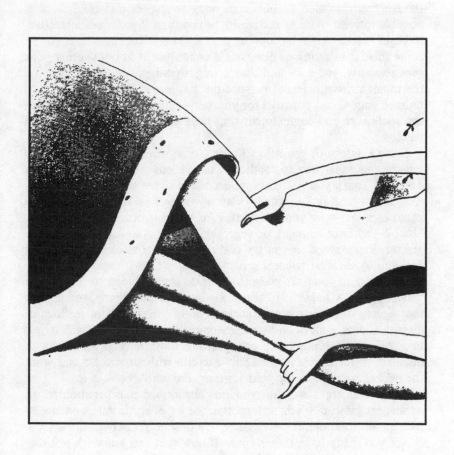

I am not convinced that a passionate, slightly bawdy, playful guide to delicious sex can easily liberate a woman from decades of prudery or negative conditioning or the kinds of deep emotional knots that inhibit sexual functioning. Nothing short of a competent therapist may help, though many women benefit from body-awareness classes. Still, it is possible to seem more attractive by behaving as if you were attractive, to begin to lose weight by copying the behavior of thin people. If you've come this far in *Delicious Sex* with a commitment to discovering your own sexuality, you may find that acting, dressing, walking, perceiving the moment from a sexual perspective may prove liberating. Learn to unleash your sexual potential for yourself—through masturbation—and the confidence and contentment that have seemed so unattainable will be closer.

Make a date with yourself. Choose a time when no one is around to interrupt and there are no conflicting obligations. Study your genitals in a mirror. Touch yourself. Explore each area to see which is most sensitive. Do your Kegel exercises. Caress yourself in all your erogenous zones as if you were your own lover (as well as your own best friend). Use oil—coconut, almond, or vegetable oil—or even saliva to keep the genital tissues moist as you try different kinds of strokes and varying pressure to see what triggers a response.

What should you feel? Warmth. Wetness inside. Blood rushing to the pelvic region. A tickle . . . the tickle intensifying. "Some women find that despite their intellectual acceptance of masturbation, feelings of disgust, shame, guilt or embarrassment persist," Lonnie Barbach writes in *For Yourself.* She advises exaggerating those feelings as a way to dissipate them. If you've tried this exercise without success and want the perfect companion for your journey, Barbach's book is it.

But if you are a woman who has abandoned masturbation as an adolescent game, or if you've forgotten the joy of erotic independence or seek an aid to a midlife renaissance, it's time to rediscover the art.

Are you ready to celebrate yourself now that you know it's not illegal, immoral, or fattening? Of course, masturbation can be fast and hot, a quick climax, a release from stress or tension, a wonderful soporific, relaxing you to sleep (and healthier than a sleeping pill). But let it be pure sensual pleasure. Unplug the telephone. Give yourself candlelight, satin sheets, music if that makes you feel sexier. Sip a glass of wine. Rub yourself with almond oil. Read a chapter from *The Story of O.* Or step into a perfumed bubble bath. Explore your body. See how the handheld shower head feels when you aim the spray at your breasts, your inner thighs, and your clitoris.

Buy a vibrator in the drugstore. Or visit a sex shop and consider a fancier model. Some women find that a vibrator moving around the clitoral area produces powerful orgasms, wave after wave exploding. For others, too-direct stimulation is unbearable, but a light touch on breasts, buttocks, thighs, and mons veneris is a surefire turn-on that fingers bring quickly to orgasm. No vibrators in the bathtub, please.

If a vibrator and steamy novels are the only sexual stimulation in your life at the moment, you might want to use the vibrator sparingly, in alternation with other masturbatory techniques. It is possible to become so addicted to the machine's intense stimulation that you lose the ability to climax any other way.

There are endless ways to masturbate—if your favorite isn't listed here, don't feel odd or abnormal. Be pleased you're so creative.

1. On your back using fingers to stimulate the clitoris and perhaps to penetrate.
2. Just visualizing a fantasy. Rare, but some women can orgasm doing it.
3. Pressing your legs together.
4. Combining clitoral stimulation and an object inside the vagina.
5. Sitting up and clenching and unclenching the Kegel-trained pubococcygeal muscle.
6. On your stomach, rubbing against the sheets or blankets or a cloth.
7. Any one or all of these combined with fantasy. If you're bored with the same old fantasy, you might leaf through Nancy Friday's *My Secret Garden* and *Forbidden Flowers.*
8. Let the jet of the Jacuzzi hit your clitoris. Even the softer flow of a swimming pool jet may be stimulating if you're skinnydipping.

Share your masturbation technique with your lover—not only will he learn what pleases you, but the experience of watching you can be highly erotic. For you both.

Remember, the best thing about masturbation when you're all alone is you don't have to look your best.

Understanding His Anatomy

Some men are so totally focused on their genitals they would think you bananas if you asked for a guide to their erogenous zones. They kiss because they've heard women like kissing. They grab and tweak and nibble and pinch, hoping to hit a magic button or two, not with any intimation of pleasure, perhaps because touches, kisses, and nibbles mean little to them—unless aimed directly between their legs at the almighty penis (plural: penes or penises—not that anyone needs two when one is this much adored). Indeed, physical affection—the kind of touching, kissing, and caressing most women hunger for—is actually disturbing to some men. It makes them uncomfortable. After a certain age, there's not much hope of freeing a man from this sad state of deprivation. You can learn to live with it if you focus on everything else that is wonderful about him. Since much of what we do for others is a reflection of what we want for ourselves, it's necessary to readjust your thinking. "I promise not to hug you if you hug me a lot," you might say.

Happily, many men are as sensitive to touch and rich in erogenous turn-on zones as the most eroticized of women, sighing, keening with pleasure, feeling shivers of excitement from lips, tongue, teeth, fingers, and firm caressing—of ears, eyelids, neck, toes, fingers, underarms, inner thighs, backs of knees, derrière. Nipples? Some seem to find nipple play annoying. Others have yet to discover the erotic potential there. But fierce, almost painful nipping and pinching is wildly exciting to still others. Indeed, most men want to be touched and caressed with more pressure than you like. Experiment. I never said this would be simple . . . just that it's worth the effort and the research is fun.

Penises differ not just in length and thickness, but also in the angle when erect, and the rhythm that brings them to orgasm. And some curl or point to the left or right. Sensitivities vary too in this erotically charged organ. Most sensitive is the head or glans, then the ridge where the glans joins the shaft, the vertical fold of skin underneath where the head connects to the shaft, and the ridge that runs down the shaft on the underside. The perineum—the area between the anus and the scrotum—is also highly erogenous, responding to firm pressure from mouth or fingers or palm. The scrotum—the sac that holds the testicles—responds to licks and kisses, to tickling and gentle caressing, to lifting and varying kinds of pressure. For many men the anus is intensely erogenous—responding to pressure and sometimes penetration. And the master gland that runs the machinery—the prostate—may have erotic power too, pressure against it helping or even triggering orgasm in some men.

The real command station—and the body's most powerful erogenous zone—is the brain, of course. And in men, the eyes rule. Men respond to visual stimulation—to beauty and to pornography and photographs that are explicitly sexual.

Women seem much less obsessed by men's bodies or physical perfection than men (another example of our natural superiority). Well, yes, there are women who obsess a bit about rippling muscles. And a tight round behind is sheer aesthetic joy. But women seem to respond more to faces, eyes, mouths—the character they reveal—the voice and what it is saying. The anatomical peculiarities of the one you love can seem enchanting. As for the unique specifications of a penis . . . women are infinitely less obsessed by that question than most men seem to be. One might confess to loving a penis that is particularly fat or remarkably firm. For every endorsement of a giant-size penis there is sure to be a complaint from a woman who just can't handle all that. I've never heard of a woman leaving a man because of the size or curve of his penis.

What may please you most about his penis is how long it stays erect, how quickly it revives after coming the first time, how happily it responds to your attentions and your pleasure, and how it reflects the passion, the tenderness, the playfulness, and the dirty mind that controls it. Indeed, the kind of stimulation most women need to climax has nothing to do with penis size. And a man with a less-than-remarkable penis may be gifted with a mouth and a tongue that take you again and again beyond ecstasy.

The Lesson of Catherine the Great

Why did Catherine the Great, Empress of all Russia, have her lovers killed after one night of sex?

Because she couldn't stand the empty feeling when a lover didn't telephone the next day.

This brilliant interpretation of history came to me one afternoon in a flash. I reported it with enthusiasm to a man friend, anticipating congratulations. He looked at me as if totally puzzled and said: "But there were no telephones in Catherine's Russia." You may also have noticed that men and women do not necessarily speak the same language at times. In sexual encounters this may be dangerous. You may be looking for love and he is on the prowl for a night of hot sex. Sometimes you feel you are dealing with a creature from outer space.

Creature	Translation
I'll call you tomorrow.	I can't wait to get out of here.
I won't come in your mouth.	Oops. Sorry. That wasn't so bad, was it?

Creature	Translation
I love you.	Whatsyername?
We'll just lie down together on top of the covers and I won't even touch you.	Was that as good for you as it was for me, baby?
My wife and I plan to divorce as soon as the children are old enough.	Old enough to be on Social Security.
I'm so hot for you tonight, darling.	If you wanted to make love you shouldn't have insisted we go dancing . . . I'm exhausted.
You've got so much to offer.	I'd like someone ten years younger and not so smart.
I'm ready to settle down now. I'm sick of the singles scene. You'll never find me in mating bars.	I'm seeing five women who adore me and you can be the sixth.
I've been secretly in love with you since you joined the company but I was afraid to say anything.	My date seems to have attached herself to someone else. I'd better find someone to spend the night with.
I've fallen in love with your eyes.	God, what incredible tits.
She's just someone I know from the office. Once in a while we have lunch together.	The wedding isn't till May. I'm entitled to one last fling.
I'm really hurt that you don't trust me. I'm only asking you up for a nightcap [to see the view from my window, taste the peach preserves my mom sent, meet my dog, etc.].	Zip.

Perhaps I am being a bit unfair. These outrageous clichés. Hardly anyone says things like this anymore. Hardly. But the truth is it's not easy being a man. All those decades when we felt it was frustrating and humiliating to be a woman, it was stressful, confusing, and terrifying to be a man. Freudian scholar Sherry Turkle puts it very well: for a boy separation from the mother is quite brutal because it happens twice— "first in the loss of the bonded infant relationship, then again at the point of Oedipal struggle."* Daughters stay close, developing a "greater capacity for empathy and a sense of self that stresses connection rather than boundaries." If some men seem angry, untrusting, afraid of intimacy and on the run, this may be why.

Understanding his different needs and fears will make you compassionate and easier to be with. The good news is that despite difficulties in communication and differing sexual responses that are probably hormonal as well as cultural, today men are saying they feel romantic, sensitive, and vulnerable. And for many men, that's true.

So don't come to me asking why it is you always fall in love with creatures from outer space.

* From the *New York Times Book Review,* May 26, 1985.

Who Wants to Play with the Aggressive Woman?

This is a chapter for the truly sexual woman, the absolutely liberated woman . . . lusty and uninhibited, comfortable initiating sex and expressing needs and desires candidly, confidently expecting her man to be happily involved in making love beyond his own orgasm.

Here you are. Don Juan's dream girl. Always ready for sex, always hot or eager to rev up the thermostat . . . a woman who almost never says no. You've read that men are always complaining that women are never sexually aggressive enough and resist erotic adventure. And you are a tigress, game for almost anything, delicately bawdy, naughty, and explicit. So why does the man in your life make you feel overwhelming and threatening?

In the not-yet-realized perfect world, sex will be a way of expressing love and affection, creating sublime pleasure, and making babies. But for now many of us use it as a marketing device or a measure of self-esteem and macho. Yes, it feels good, and it also makes us feel good—it's a score, a notch on the belt, a real sense of accomplishment. That's why, with all the serious talk about not playing games anymore, we still seem to put special value on the man or woman who is hard to get and a woman who is too easy to bed is still an object of contempt.

Don Juan's overaggressiveness should be suspect. The deep insecurity that keeps him on the prowl makes him particularly vulnerable to the aggressive woman. He may be uncomfortable if he cannot be the one who decides when and where you will make love and how and what games you will play. What feels like healthy lust to you may seem like a constant demand for performance to him. His idea of a wholesomely aggressive woman is someone who responds like crazy and initiates once in a while.

You've come a long way, baby, but we still have a long way to go before sexual gender roles blur and homogenize. A man doesn't have to be a pathological Don Juan to feel threatened by overt aggressiveness in a woman. Many of the bright, loving, sensitive, consciousness-raised men you and I have fallen/will fall for need a sense of conquest. Your pleasure is not just your pleasure . . . it's his accomplishment. And a drill sergeant's voice coming from your pouty lips crying: "Harder, faster . . . no, not like that, damm it . . . give it to me like a real man . . . pretend you like it"—is sure to be highly antierotic. Too-fast ejaculation, the disappearing erection, and sexual boredom are his way to control your demands.

A healthy, sexually mature, confident man is your perfect bedmate. He will respond to your aggressiveness and get aroused by your playfulness—happy to share the physical pleasure and your connection as lovers. But if you are involved—perhaps rather contentedly—with an incurable chauvinist or an unreformable adolescent, my advice is: be gentle. Flirt. Don't stun him with a direct attack. I can't imagine a man so confident he doesn't warm to real encouragement.

On first meeting:

HE:	I feel that I know you from somewhere.
YOU:	They call that precognition. It means you *want* to know me.
HE:	Oh, really?
YOU (A):	That woman I saw you talking to . . . if you tell me she's your wife, I'm moving to Montana tomorrow.
YOU (B):	Come into the closet with me and I'll show you what I mean.

On a first date:

HE:	Why do you eat your salad with your fingers?
YOU:	I like to be in touch with everything I do.
HE:	You certainly have a lot of confidence.
YOU (A):	Then why do I feel weak at the knees when you look at me like that?
YOU (B):	Let's skip dessert and go to a hotel.

First night in bed:

HE:	I want to make you crazy. I want to do everything you love.
YOU (A):	Give me your mouth. (Kissing him.) That's the perfect beginning.
YOU (B):	Stop talking and touch me here.

If you are a B personality, you risk terrifying your man. Vulnerable as he seems, he could be a candidate for consciousness-raising if you go slowly. He might even be a contender for long-term commitment if your need to be direct and earthy doesn't frighten him away.

The Renaissance of Foreplay

The Sexual Revolution has not been kind to foreplay. Sport Sex and Playful Sex and Sex-for-Its-Own-Sake made it so easy to hop into bed that some folks practically abandoned hugging and kissing and soulful caressing and silly fooling around. Great lovers and serious sensualists never gave up foreplay. Indeed, it was Casanova who said his hottest moments were as he climbed the stairs to her bedroom. (This book does not accept that anticipation is hotter than realization, but we weren't around to coach Casanova.)

Foreplay embraces all the erotic innuendoes and dialogue, the subliminal body language and the caressing, the hugging and sucking and kissing and stroking that precede actual intercourse. "Everything but," as they used to say in the innocent sixties. Foreplay keeps your fingers and mouth happy and your blood rushing as you flirt, explore each other's ideas and values, see how your two biological clocks work together, whether your neuroses can mesh—till you make a commitment to go all the way.

Usually it's the woman who choses the moment, even in these post-liberation times. But sometimes the man will surprise you, murmuring that he needs to know you better . . . cooling the pace, prolonging the foreplay. Endless postponement is probably never quite so intensely exciting as when the two of you take turns putting off the first consummation long after you are both longing for it desperately, long after you both know it is inevitable. Keeping yourself and your man at a fever pitch for hours or days or weeks, even months, is exquisite torture.

Once you're actually sharing a bed, a bedroom, and the rent, foreplay may become an elusive luxury. Unless you make time for it. Provoke it. Insist on it. Invent new rituals. Support the revival of foreplay. Exercise: Explore Ford Play, Fork Play, Floor Play, Fjord Play. (See pages 52–70.)

Dear Ann Landers: Hungry for Hugs, Kissing Is Wonderful Too

There just aren't enough hugs going around. Ann Landers shocked everyone when she reported on a survey of American women, asked what they would choose if they were offered sex or a cuddle. They desperately wanted to cuddle. A good way to get more hugs is to hug and be huggable. There are people, most of them male, I suspect, who are acutely uncomfortable being touched (except sexually). It's so neurotic that I don't want to delve deeply into this aberration at a stage when you need a full measure of positive energy. If your man hates to be touched, you probably know it and you have decided, or will, that you can live with the reality because you want him or need him and he's wonderful in one hundred other ways.

But if he's just shy or awkward or needs encouragement, your warmth and easy-flowing affection may be all he needs. If he's used to grabbing sex on the run, he may not understand your appetite for long kissing, body-to-body melting hugs, and the erotic potential of caressing. Go with your feeling, snuggling against him in the taxi, taking his arm on the street, caressing the back of his neck and wrapping your fingers in the curls at the nape; rub into him. Give him your lips, lick his just a little, kiss his neck. Open your eyes. Smile. Your body—rigid and arched back or curious, open, and right there—speaks of your affection, your tenderness and curiosity, your growing excitement, or your need to cool it. Give the message you really want to give: "I like you." "I feel playful." "I'm unbelievably hot for you."

If he's not a dedicated kisser—not even a good kisser—don't despair. Show him how a great kisser kisses. Kiss him the way you want to be kissed. (See "69 Ways to Turn You On," pages 77–82, and "69 Ways to Turn Him On," pages 83–86.) Don't just stand there like a department-store mannequin. Kiss him. Kiss him back. Kiss him first. If the kisses are getting better and you don't want to stop, be encouraging: "I need to kiss you a lot." "I want to kiss you all over." "We have so much time. I won't go away." "Kissing like this makes me unbelievably hot." "Come here. I want to feel you next to me." "You have the best mouth."

And when your kisses have explored every possibility of your mouths, there are hundreds of other erogenous landing fields. What's nice about kissing is that there are no rules. It can be creative and improvisational. Some couples will get to know each other's bodies intimately in foreplay—perhaps long before consummation. It is also possible that the two of you have to make love first—from first tentative kisses to coitus and orgasm—before you develop the physical intimacy to explore each other's bodies and sensual responses. Lazy loving afternoons, with soft light filtered through gauzy curtains or bright sun toasting your bodies through an open window, are perfect for tracing the outline of his body, reading the textures of his skin as you would Braille, asking where the scar on his knee comes from, discovering what strokes and pressures make him purr, make him gasp, make him moan. Washing each other in the bath, toweling each other dry, powdering each other all over permit more playful exploration.

Verbal Foreplay— Words that Sound Hot

Some words are intrinsically hot without being explicitly sexual. Your own provocative inflection—or a sideways glance, a teasing smile—can transform an innocent word into an erotic intimation. Exercise: Study early Lauren Bacall and vintage Garbo movies.

Hot Words

skin	peach	chocolate	carnal
mouth	musk	hunger	vixen
mango	spicy	inside	voluptuous
wet	indulgence	roseate	scarlet
creamy	naked	pubescent	shameless
velvet	naughty	torrid	hot-blooded
asterisk*	succulent	jalapeño†	radiant
wanton	violet	silken	body heat
rush	Maserati	incalescence	sultry
sticky	indigo	electric blanket	blazing
fettuccine	animal	intimation	

* Especially inflaming to a philologist.
† Incendiary to Tex-Mex aficionados.

Ford Play— Warming Up in Cars, Taxis, and Limousines

Not so long ago, in the days before bucket seats and seat-belt laws, the automobile was an erotic playpen. Inhibited by anxious parents and a strict double standard for sexual behavior, "nice" girls made out like crazy in parked cars, and some boasted of moving violations. A car had just one tufted expanse of front seat—rather like a living-room sofa—and you could be teasing or daring, possessive and intimate, just by putting your hand on his thigh or sitting glued to his side. A few really old-fashioned buggies still had the shift stick on the floor, and to get close you had to put the stick between your legs. That was outrageously sexy, too.

Ford play is still hot. Autos shelter intense snuggling and other erotic love play these days, but you have to be a contortionist to feel each other up below the seat belt without unbuckling. Anyway, I'm definitely not recommending it at fifty-five miles an hour. Park if you feel like being seriously lewd.

The moving roadster is still a fine place for foreplay, verbal and kinetic. If you haven't made out in a car for decades, give it a try. Park anywhere. If it's winter your heat will steam the windshields and give you privacy. Necking and groping are joys that should not be abandoned to adolescents.

Ford play in a taxi. Strictly legal and no holds barred except what you don't want observed by the driver. Or is that half the fun?

Ford play in a limousine. This is really grownup stuff—making out like teenagers on cushy suede upholstery with a bar, TV, and the tinted windows or shades rolled down to foil voyeurs so you can make love between business meetings or on the way home from lunch. Perhaps instead of lunch. The mobile car phone makes it possible to thrill a friend with an obscene phone call from you as he moves downtown in traffic.

Advanced ford play. Find a deserted country road or a jeep trail into a wood. Having aroused yourselves with dialogue, you'll be ready to make love fully dressed while leaning against the fender. Or, for his birthday, hire a stretch limo with cassette player and pour a bottle of ice-cold bubbly. Take him to dinner and dancing and then around the park as often as you like.

Fork Play

BEGINNING FORK PLAY— SEDUCTION IN RESTAURANTS

He seems endlessly polite, reserved, and hopelessly superficial. Here you two are in a cozy little corner, dining by candlelight, sipping a warming California Cabernet, and all he wants to talk about is the Dow-Jones, gabardines, tax planning, and the latest scandal in the daily newspaper. You want to make the conversation more intimate but not provocative to the point of no return. You don't want to frighten him. He may be shy or wary, bitter or wounded from his last romance, eager for love and terrified all at once.

Here's where you can be a diplomat, investigative reporter, and seductress while ingesting the evening's ration of minerals and vitamins (hopefully, delicious). Remember, your questions may be brilliant but you can't be sure his answers are honest. Still, even lies and evasions can be revealing. You might ask:

1. What do you do when you're not doing what you're paid to do?
2. What's your idea of the most fun you can possibly have on a Saturday afternoon . . . on a four-day weekend?
3. If money and time weren't an issue, where would you spend the summer?

4. Are you a breakfast-in-bed person? Or do you have to get up and brush your teeth first?
5. Do your kids take after you?
6. What do you think are your best qualities . . . and the worst?
7. What is the best gift anyone ever gave you?
8. Does it upset you when people respond to you for qualities that seem unimportant to you?
9. Are you a cook?
10. Do you trust restaurant critics?
11. Are you and your ex-wife good friends?
12. What is your closest friend like?
13. Do you still see your friends from high school?
14. If you were starting all over again today, would you choose the same occupation?
15. If you knew you were going to die six months from today, without any illness or pain, what would you do in your last six months?
16. Where would you like to be five years from today? What would you like to have accomplished?
17. Would you say you've ever been in love?
18. Do you think nature meant for man to be married?
19. If you were left with a huge trust fund tomorrow, would you stop working?

Any one or more of these questions can move the conversation to a level of real intimacy and give you a sense of his values and tastes. Remember, this is not the interrogation of a political prisoner in a totalitarian state—don't pounce.

How he eats is revealing, too. Does he prefer white meat to dark, white wine to red? Is he reluctant to order fish on the bone? Does he leave half the lamb chop rather than pick it up, or tear at a huge veal chop with his teeth? Does he guzzle the wine or savor it? Does he seem disturbed that you eat salad with your fingers? When you lick your fingers, does he seem embarrassed or does he offer to help? I've always believed that men who don't eat ice cream probably hate sand, sleep in pajamas, and kiss with their mouths closed. Happily, there are men whose sexuality defies their prissy eating habits. One of my best lovers ever was a white-meat-white-wine-no-bones man, and when he suddenly picked up a whole chicken breast with both hands and got grease on his chin at dinner, I knew he'd never stop pleasing me. And he never did.

INTERMEDIATE FORK PLAY— MORE SEDUCTION IN RESTAURANTS

You have the feeling tonight is the night. He is the man for you. You know it. But perhaps he needs more convincing. Or you just want to use the hours at dinner to heighten the pitch of excitement. Choose the phrases that truly apply, and be prepared to explain what you mean if he asks.

1. I feel so safe with you.
2. Does it bother you that I can't seem to keep my hands off you?
3. No, I don't always wear stockings with seams, but tonight I want especially to please you.
4. You're the first man I've met in so long whom I want to see again and again.
5. Am I crazy? I can't seem to stop smiling when I'm with you.
6. I love the way you smell.
7. It isn't fair that you're handsomer than any other man in the room.
8. I keep wondering if you can possibly be as good a lover as you are a dancer.
9. I can't concentrate all day (or, better, I get twice as much done in a day) when I know that I'm seeing you later.
10. I was exhausted when I got home from the office tonight, but I took a long hot bath with bubbles and a twenty-minute nap and I feel like I was just born.
11. Can you concentrate on dinner if I touch you here? Here? Oh dear . . . may I touch that?
12. I'm so happy it's Saturday and we don't have to think about tomorrow.
13. No, I don't always carry a nightgown in the pocket of my coat

but for some reason I brought it tonight . . . are you superstitious?

14. If I asked you to go under the table and make love to me, would you?

15. I have an invitation for a party tonight at a disco, unless you'd rather just come home with me for a brandy and some great jazz.

Don't worry if some of this dialogue is too outrageous for you. Your body speaks. Without even thinking, you lean forward . . . toward him, open. Your fingers play with the stem of your glass. You do not notice how you touch yourself—your wrist, your neck, a finger on your lip, at your neckline, toying with a thin gold chain, your tongue licking the wine goblet, biting the edge of the glass. Every gesture telegraphs your invitation, your sensuality—the appealing nervous edge of your excitement.

ADVANCED FORK PLAY— RESTAURANT OUTRAGEOUSNESS

Dinner out when it's just the two of you ought to be romantic even if you're longtime mates. You can make it special by feeling hot—doing wonderful things to your body in the tub, choosing the underwear that turns *you* on, the outer look that turns him on, switching bags (from serious to frivolous) and earrings (neat to sparkly) and makeup (daylight to a luminescent glow). (Men who like the way their wives look make love more often and are more satisfied with their sex lives.) Imagine it's a date and he is someone you scarcely know. Spare him the depressing news from home—zero balance in the bank account, failing report cards, ornery carpenters, autos ticketed and towed away. Be amusing. Talk about something you've never discussed before. Be discreetly lewd (not drunk and disorderly, just mischievous). For ideas you might rent *Flashdance, Tom Jones, Shampoo,* and the porn flick *The Story of Joanna* to see what kind of exhibitionism and teasing is possible at dinner.

Try one or two of the gambits below. I wouldn't try all of them at

once. He might get so annoyed he could smash you in the face with a cantaloupe.

I love what you did to me this morning.

Whenever I think of last night I get so hot I can't sit still.

Do you think we could make a porn movie tonight?

Do you come here often? I don't think I've ever seen you before.

My exercise teacher is mad about your ass . . . do you think I have the courage to share you with her?

Could we skip dessert and go immediately to the nearest hotel?

Would you meet me downstairs in the telephone booth? I want to feel you up.

You are amazing . . . it's a shame you can't teach a sex class for young men who want to be great lovers. You know things no one else knows.

I'm going to give you my phone number. But I don't want any more of your dirty obscene phone calls . . . except tonight.

Pick out any woman in this room and tell me what we would do to her if we took her home with us.

When you left the house this morning for work I rolled over into your warm spot on the bed and played with myself while thinking of you.

Tell me a hot bedtime story.

I want to play Doctor . . . I think you have a fever and I will cure it. Give me your hand.

The hatcheck girl is smiling at me. If I invite her home, will you teach me how to make love to a woman?

AT HOME—MENUS FOR FIFTEEN-MINUTE SUPPERS BEFORE SEX

Foolish eating and drinking before love is clearly antiaphrodisiacal. So don't get caught up in impressing your man with your culinary skill —trotting out too many wines you have cleverly tucked away in your cellar or broom closet, then capping the evening with a rare old Cognac. Save the gourmandisiacal hijinks for breakfast. That way you can lull him back to sleep and start the day again in midafternoon with more sex.

What do great sex and great food have in common? Each makes you ravenous for more. They are two of life's unsurpassed sensual thrills. And while some people repress their sex drive by overeating and gastronomic obsession, others use sex as a way to distract themselves from food. "Make love instead" is the motto one of my friends has taped to her refrigerator door. What a delightful cure for the insatiable munchies.

Food and sex have another crucial link. The same neural transmitter, norepinephrine, carries the sensory messages of eating and making love. The same neural link registers the crunch of celery, the chiaroscuro of an Oreo cookie, the smell of a young Beaujolais, the curve of your lover's mouth, the scent of his hair.

What should you drink? Just a little. Beginners will feel energized and romantic sipping champagne. Wine connoisseurs will be moved and warmed by a really great vintage—keep a few half bottles for a splurge that's alcoholically prudent. Most people equate rich sauces and pasta with heaviness, red meat with virility. A demitasse of high voltage could be just the caffeine kick he needs to keep him awake for whatever else you have in mind tonight.

Menus for Supper Before Sex—
The Fifteen-Minute Gourmand

For an Epicure

Scrambled eggs with white truffles
The best salad greens you can find in a mustardy vinaigrette
Chocolate Wickedness (from your freezer; see page 65)
Raspberries
A half bottle of a great California Cabernet Sauvignon—'74, '76, '78
    —Jordan, Mondavi, Stag's Leap, Sterling, Simi, Mayacammas,
    Beaulieu Private Reserve

For a He-Man

Ground chunk or sirloin; add a tablespoon of cream and a teaspoon
    of grated onion; sauté in butter
Great tomatoes (if it's the season) sprinkled with olive oil, a few
    drops of vinegar, salt, freshly cracked pepper, and snipped basil;
    romaine and watercress in vinaigrette if the tomatoes are not
    sweet off the vine
Brownies with a scoop of chocolate chip ice cream and hot fudge
    sauce
Good beer or a half bottle of Barolo

Supper on a Restricted Budget

Quickly seared chicken livers with caramelized onions and a dab of
    sour cream
Salad of orange segments, fennel slivers, and walnuts in a mild olive
    oil vinaigrette
Mocha almond fudge ice cream
A half bottle of a small Bordeaux from a good year

A Very Light Supper

Sea scallops, shaken in a paper bag with bread crumbs, a little salt,
   and fresh pepper, then sautéed in brown butter very quickly till
   crisp on the outside, just barely warm within
Julienne of zucchini or cucumber or slivers of endive cooked in butter
   with a dash of lemon and a shake of ground cumin or any fresh
   herb: terragon, mint, coriander, even parsley
Fresh figs (see page 23) with whipped cream or crème fraîche
A chocolate truffle
Half a bottle of Saint Veran or Mâcon blanc

AFTER-LOVE SNACKS

Great sex can make you hungry for more. Sometimes it just makes
you hungry. Or it makes you lazy and languorous and leaves him ravenous.

That's when you need ice cream, Chocolate Wickedness (see page
65), and candy bars in the freezer . . . the makings of instant pasta in
the fridge, beautiful fruit, yogurt . . . a nice long-lasting salami. If
you've planned ahead and tucked away the makings of an after-love
eating binge, you can dream away. He'll just help himself.

BREAKFAST BEFORE OR AFTER
LOVE

Some men really prefer sex in the morning after a good eight hours'
sleep. That's when testosterone is the highest. Some men wake up with
a morning erection—and it's a shame to just waste it. If he seems hesi-
tant, not sure how receptive you'll be, you might nuzzle against him or
reach out and stroke it. You can pretend you're responding though still
deep asleep. Some men rather like sort of sneaking up on a helpless,
indifferent woman. You might enjoy the fantasy too. Set the alarm fif-

teen minutes earlier than you need to and allow for a fast, hot . . . you know what.

But if it's Saturday or Sunday (and you've farmed out the kids or taught them to respect your mornings, or bribed roommates to stay away), it's a luxury to linger in bed for breakfast. One of you will have to make it. Flip a coin. If the tray is already set up in the kitchen and the makings are handy, he might be pleased to indulge you at least half the time.

Breakfast in Bed for Neophyte Cooks

Croissants warmed in the toaster oven
Butter and great jam
Beautiful fruit
Freshly squeezed orange juice
Coffee or tea

Breakfast in Bed for Wantons

Fresh imported beluga caviar or fresh salmon roe
A bagel sliced in three horizontally, toasted
Crème fraîche or sour cream or cream cheese
Butter and apricot preserves
Russian coffee cake
Coffee or tea

Easy Breakfast in Bed

Smoked salmon
Lemon quarters
Seriously glorious fruit, preferably great berries
Cream cheese, great French cheese
Black bread
Coffee or tea

Sentimental Breakfast in Bed

Brioche or challah sliced thick and made into French toast
Real maple syrup or cherry preserves
Freshly squeezed grapefruit juice
Coffee or tea

Low-Fat Breakfast for Special Cases

Broiled grapefruit with brown sugar glaze
Low-fat yogurt with sliced banana and berries, or a toasted bagel,
    thinly sliced, with low-fat cottage cheese or ricotta, creamed
    smooth and blended with minced chives, scallions, or fresh herbs
Espresso

FOOD AS A SEX TOY

Some people enjoy dipping or smearing each other with syrupy,
sticky food and then licking it off. This is not an absolutely authoritative
or all-inclusive list, but delicacies one hears recommended for sex play
are:

Whipped cream
Hot fudge sauce (not too hot, please)
Peanut butter
Strawberry preserves
Honey
A banana
Grapes
Chocolate éclair
Popsicles (on a very sultry afternoon)

Improvisation would seem to be the guiding spirit. As a food purist
and a sex purist the concept here seems perverse to me, but for some

people daubing each other with food is good clean fun (if gooey), and for others perversity is part of the pleasure. A man I know always wanted to make love in a bathtub full of gelatin. The plumbing wasn't right for weeks after.

There is a scene of submissive love play in the movie *9½ Weeks* in which the man blindfolds the woman naked in front of an open refrigerator and feeds her a cherry, a love tomato, honey (all over her face), and finally a whole jalapeño pepper. Twice. This is definitely advanced fork play . . . a kind of edible sadomasochism.

APHRODISIACS

Science says there are no aphrodisiacs, except Spanish fly. But rumors persist. Ginseng, black truffles, powdered rhinoceros horn, and turtle blood are folklore favorites. Marquesan men rub themselves with turmeric, which sounds like tumescence and may be worth a try. Perhaps Casanova knew what he was doing, putting away dozens of oysters every morning—oysters are rich in zinc, essential for sperm and male hormone.

The Aztecs believed chocolate would inflame men with passion. Montezuma guzzled chocolatl—a cold, bitter cacao brew—before returning to his harem. I've always suspected chocolate has aphrodisiacal power. Certainly I have done my best to spread the rumor. There is a strong element of mind over matter in questions of potency—if you believe it works, it works. I'm so sure, I always keep a jarful of deep, dark, mysterious Chocolate Wickedness in my freezer. And chocolate does contain phenylethylamine, a chemical humans manufacture when they're in love. Whip up a batch. Share it with a chocoholic. Suddenly you're not merely a sex object and a brilliant person, you're a sorceress.

Chocolate Wickedness

A variation on a recipe from Paula Peck's *The Art of Fine Baking*.

1½ pounds semisweet chocolate
4 egg yolks

½ cup espresso coffee
½ cup crème de cacao
8 egg whites
Pinch of salt
¼ cup sugar
1 cup heavy cream, whipped

Melt the chocolate in a heavy saucepan over water. Add the egg yolks, espresso, and crème de cacao. Stir together till smooth. (If the mixture hardens, warm gently and stir till smooth. Then let cool.) Beat the egg whites with salt till they hold soft peaks. Add the sugar, a tablespoon at a time, beating after each addition. Continue beating 5 more minutes, or until stiff. Fold the whipped cream into the egg whites and then fold in the chocolate mixture. Pour into a large glass bowl or a soufflé dish with a waxed-paper collar (or covered jar if it's just for late-night fixes) and store in the freezer until 15 minutes before serving. (It's great frozen, too.) If you have time to be fancy, serve with a sauce made by blending 1 cup heavy cream, whipped into soft peaks, with ½ cup sour cream and 1 teaspoon vanilla extract.

True Aphrodisiacs Are

Great sex
Morning—that's all it takes to give some men erections
Exercise and good nutrition
A new partner
Candy panties (sold in some sex shops)

Floor Play— Love on the Dance Floor

Dancing can ignite sexual fire. Doing anything you do well with your body is exciting to watch, and a real high for you, too—just feeling yourself dazzle and skip beyond the edge of exhaustion. Have you noticed how some disco dancing is hot and some is not? Stand on the edge of a dance floor. You'll see what I mean. You can be cute or athletic, you can be ladylike and sadly constricted, or you can move with a subtle, seductive, animal spirit.

Dancing close up is even hotter . . . especially when you both have the same message. The lights are low. You have lost all inhibition. Everyone else fades away as you two move against each other, knees invading, creating erotic friction . . . perhaps even a climax on the dance floor. At least you're both candidates for a fast hop home to a quick shower—another spot for arousing foreplay.

Going with the heat of the moment means a dark corner, and any floor will do. Advanced floor play means you don't wait when you are both turned on. Behind the living-room door, your fur coat thrown on the library floor, on the Ping-Pong table in the rec room or an exercise mat in the sauna. Don't give your heat a chance to cool. Go with it . . . wherever you are.

Fjord Play—
Alfresco Love and
Other Amusements

Fjord play is most authentic with a Scandinavian, of course. I mention it as a reminder that alfresco foreplay is always exciting—in the hammock, on the beach, half hidden in a sand dune, on the ski lift.

Here are additional variations of foreplay you may or may not wish to explore:

Fur play—foreplay on a fur coat

Flog play—sadistic foreplay

Flawed play—fooling around when your heart isn't quite in it

Fraud play—pretending you had an orgasm when you didn't; pretending you didn't have an orgasm when you did

Fog play—flirting and fooling around with someone while trying to remember if you went all the way with him the last time

Four play—two couples warming up in hopes of an orgy and possible intracross

Frog play—having carnal knowledge of frogs' legs Provençal; also, kissing a frog in the hope he will turn into a prince

Forced play—being tied up and coerced into foreplay

Fare play—kissing someone in the hope he'll loan you the price of a subway token or a round-trip air fare

Foul play—hugging and kissing without taking a bath
Fowl play—petting over a bowl of homemade chicken soup
Forensic play—intimacies with a lawyer
Forehead play—a very strange fetish
Foreign play—fooling around with an illegal alien

P.S. Beware of Try-Sexuals—someone who will try anything. Buy-Sexuals—who can climax only while shopping. Pan-Sexuals—who sublimate their sexual urges in gourmet cooking.

Turn Yourself On

There are nights when everything conspires to make you hot. His voice. The promise in your dialogue at dinner. The memory of the last time you were together. His fingers against your lips. The pressure of your knee against his. Your fantasies of what will happen when you are alone at last. You are flushed and high, hot and wet. The teasing and foreplay might go on for hours. You cannot imagine being hotter or wetter.

This readiness for lovemaking is a state you can recreate for yourself whenever you wish. If you've come this far, embraced the philosophy of sexual confidence and done all your sensuality exercises, you have the knowledge and ought to be in touch with the images and rituals that fuel this heat for you. How simple to use your brain to turn yourself on. And yet few men and women deliberately work to arouse themselves. Everything we learn about sex tells us we have to focus on exciting our mate.

One of the leading male actors in porn films was asked how he was able to perform sexually when the script required him to make love to someone he didn't particularly care for. "I put myself in the mood," he said, "just as any actor does." Few of us consciously try to put ourselves in the mood. Most of us climb into bed at night with our partner and wait for his aggressive lovemaking to warm the blood. A knowing caress or even the shock of sudden roughness will strike a sexual response or, feeling loving and willing, we turn with a gesture and a mouth that knows where his hunger is. Distracted, perhaps, not really as dedicated to the greatness of the moment as the legendary porn star with cameras rolling, we wait for the specific act that will get the blood rushing. Try deliberately blotting out mundane thoughts that clutter the brain at bedtime, and fill it instead with erotic newsreels, the images you can use to build the heat so that finally pleasure takes over.

"It's flattering to think just being with me all evening has made her wet," one accomplished lover confides. "I hate the feeling that a woman is lying there waiting to see what I'll do to turn it on . . . if I can turn her on."

This is not to say a woman should walk around advertising her perpetual state of sexual arousal. Living with someone who is always turned on can become a tyranny too—making it impossible ever to surprise, cajole, or seduce or feel any hint of challenge. But if you will take charge of your own sexual arousal from time to time and you know exactly what it takes to build the intensity to climax, you can be responsible for your orgasm too. A tired lover, a distracted lover . . . a less-than-inspired lover . . . it won't matter.

If you take the responsibility, your pleasure is guaranteed. Because you know your sexual needs so well, your timing, your rhythm, your desire for clitoral stimulation, you can adjust your position to make whatever he does work for you. You can rub your clitoris against his shin or knee or foot as your mouth makes love to his penis. When you're riding on top, his pubic bone can provide intense clitoral friction. If he's on top, your exercise-toned and strengthened torso can arrange an angle to make it work for you too. When you open your legs to him and he doesn't touch, you can caress yourself. He may get the idea and discover he wants to help. And now that you've found your mysterious G-spot, you can entice him into positions that favor it, thrust against him if he's too gentle. And once he realizes how you have lessened your demand on him, he may feel freer, more relaxed, less weary, rejuvenated.

Yes, a skilled and loving lover can take you to heights of sexuality you never dreamed possible, but knowing what you know and loving sex more every day, you can get to the far side of ecstasy all on your own, with almost any functioning bedmate as a reasonably willing co-conspirator.

A Treasure Chart to Help You Find Your G-Spot

A passionate case has been made for the existence inside every woman of a small patch of tissue on the front wall of the vagina, about two inches or so from the entrance, that is extremely sensitive to intense pressure. When properly stimulated—the key is intense pressure—this tissue, fondly referred to as the G-spot after Dr. Ernest Grafenberg, its original discoverer, leads to orgasm or a series of orgasms in some women and reportedly to ejaculation of a liquid similar to male ejaculate in a few women.

This finding is a serious blow to the theory that all orgasms require clitoral stimulation. But it's great news for women. Sex therapists' careers may be riding on this debate, but for most women an orgasm is an orgasm is an orgasm, and the more the merrier. While the experts argue whether or not such a divine vaginal landscape is possible, adventurous lovers have already found it. Or now some women have an explanation for why hard thrusting in certain positions creates such exquisite pleasure. And those women who do shoot fluid at orgasm (which has none of the characteristics of urine) now know they are not alone, although perhaps quite rare.

Can firm pressure on the G-spot produce orgasm? Some women insist it does. Exercises: Locate your G-spot and make it happy. By yourself,

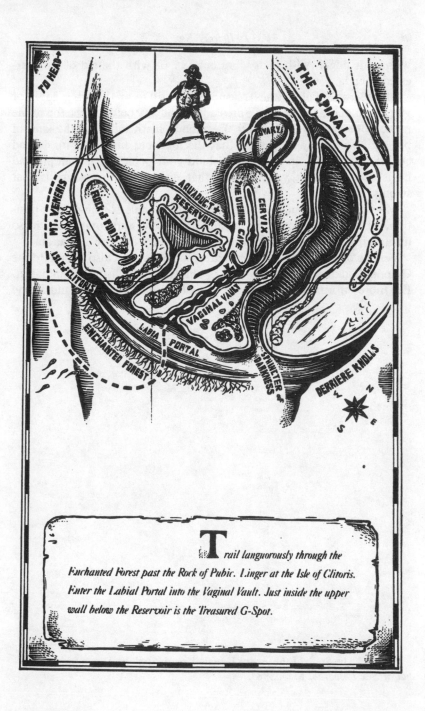

Trail languorously through the Enchanted Forest past the Rock of Pubic. Linger at the Isle of Clitoris. Enter the Labial Portal into the Vaginal Vault. Just inside the upper wall below the Reservoir is the Treasured G-Spot.

with your finger, with your vibrator . . . or with the aid of an interested friend.

Method #1. Follow the Treasure Chart till your thrusting finger or
vibrator touches this sensitive area about halfway between the top of the
pubic bone and the cervix. Dr. Desmond Heath indicates the kind of
pressure needed by suggesting that the man put his finger inside and
curl it, so that the tip is hooked behind your pubic bone, then pretend
he is about to pick you up with that finger. "The pressure is that
strong," he says.*

Method #2. Arrange yourself and mate in male-spoons-female position, let him enter you from behind and below, and rotate your torso
until hard thrusting produces an excruciatingly exciting sensation.

Female on top and other rear-entry positions may also stimulate the
G-spot. Looking for your G-spot is almost as much fun as finding it.
For more information, read *The G-Spot* by Ladas, Whipple, and Perry.

---

* From "The State of the Art of Female Ejaculation" by Dawn Stover, *Journal of Sex Research,* May, 1984.

69 Ways
to Turn You On

You may want to rip out these pages and leave them where he can't miss them.

1. Kissing. Soft lips. Romantic kissing.
2. A compliment. Something extravagant that he really means.
3. Kissing. Kissing your neck and earlobes. Kissing your eyelids. Kissing the hollows of your clavicles.
4. Looking at you as if he adores you (but not if he doesn't really).
5. Reading to you. His favorite stories. His favorite poems.
6. Sending you flowers because it's Tuesday.
7. Necking in the car.
8. Pressing your cheeks with both hands as he kisses you.
9. Kissing. Kissing the corners of your mouth. Teasing bites. Invasive kisses.
10. Letting you undress him.
11. Undressing you slowly and making love to each part as it appears.
12. Slow dancing naked to the radio.
13. A long indulgent erotic massage.
14. Kissing. Kissing your fingers. Your palm. Kissing the pulse in-

side your wrist. Sucking your fingers. Licking between each finger.

15. Bringing you a glass of champagne in the bathtub and a towel he has warmed in front of the fireplace (or on the radiator).

16. Playing with your breasts and thighs and clitoris with a massaging shower head.

17. Being very forceful. Kissing you roughly. Throwing you over the back of a chair and kissing your ass and pressing his palm against your whole genital area, especially the clitoris, without removing your panties.

18. Telling you what to do. Making you tell him what he is doing to you. His insisting you use all the four-letter words.

19. Pressing his thigh up against your genital area. Holding your hands over your head as if you're being forced.

20. Kissing. Kissing your breasts, your nipples, under your breasts. Appreciating your breasts verbally. In a poem. With his hands. With his fingertips. With his cheeks. Stroking, holding, pressure up to the point where it ceases to be pleasure . . . you'll let him know.

21. Nibbling. Licking. Sucking. Less-than-serious biting.

22. Carrying you anywhere. Gracefully. Especially to bed.

23. Kissing the bottoms of your feet and your instep, massaging your feet. Sucking your toes.

24. Kissing a flower and then using it to trace the outline of your nakedness, to open your legs, to stroke your nipples and clitoris.

25. Kissing. Kissing your stomach. Your belly button (if you aren't too ticklish). Kissing where the bones go in, where the bones go out. Loving your mons veneris. Kissing your inner thighs and behind the knees.

26. Loving your smells. The sun on your skin. Your after-the-bath-smell. Your perfume. Your sweet vaginal scent. Your hot vaginal musk.

27. Asking you to masturbate while he watches . . . becoming part of what you do in self-arousal.

28. Kissing. Kissing the deepest insides of your thighs and vulva. Breathing on your clitoris. Circling all around it with gentle strokes. Kissing around it. Touching it gently. Pulling the skin around it. Sucking it. Alternating just barely grazing it with

pressure. Tiny nips. Gently. Flicking it with his tongue from side to side. Burying his face there.

29. His obvious pleasure in your taste.

30. Telling you he has a delicious surprise for you just as he kisses you with your juices still on his lips.

31. Making up a bedtime story with you as the heroine.

32. His telling you everything he thinks is truly wondrous about you. What he's heard. What he's discovered. That all the women formerly number one in his life are jealous of you.

33. His never asking you if you like this or that but paying attention, and if you don't . . . his stopping.

34. Spanking you a little. Not seriously, unless you seem to like it.

35. If you're the best at anything, telling you.

36. Letting you know when you please him. Sometimes letting you know in writing—the next morning, delivered by a messenger with blueberry muffins.

37. His looking at you from time to time as he kisses you . . . as he eats you.

38. Adoring your feet. Caressing your instep under the table at the Four Seasons. Taking off your shoe and pressing your foot into his crotch so you can tease his cock with your toes.

39. Feeding you.

40. Telling you what he plans to do to you later.

41. Telling you what he is fantasizing doing to you at this very moment as he speaks to you by telephone and insisting you tell what the conversation is doing to you, because it's making him hot and crazy.

42. Making love to you in the taxi . . . exposing your panties and garter belt to the driver.

43. When the two of you are away for a weekend together, his writing you a postcard and mailing it, telling you how happy he was to be with you.

44. Sharing your bath or shower. Making love to you with the soap, the washcloth, his hands, his mouth. Drying you with the towel, splashing talcum powder and perfume all over.

45. Never thinking he's told you enough how wonderful you are. (If he means it, too much is never enough.)

46. If he can't keep his hands off you . . . he shouldn't. Naturally,

he would never embarrass you. As the waiter leads you to your table, no one can see his hand on your ass.

47. Shoving you into a dark doorway. Kissing you and feeling you up.

48. Making love to you in movie theaters, elevators, men's rooms, on the Vaporetto in Venice, on the deuxième étage of the Eiffel Tower, in Bloomingdale's lingerie department.

49. Buying you the panties he wants you to wear.

50. Asking you to model them.

51. Buying you a silly toy.

52. Buying you a sex toy.

53. Hugging you a lot . . . languorous skin-to-skin hugging in bed, hugging you close after sex, falling asleep tucked into each other.

54. Bringing you breakfast in bed on a tray, sharing the croissant and tropical fruit, then putting the tray on the floor and making love.

55. Skipping work and spending his day in bed with you. (It's not quite as impressive if he does this on a weekend, but it wouldn't be sneered at.)

56. Letting you have three or four orgasms before you start intercourse.

57. Playing with you afterward till you have four or five or six more.

58. Not stopping till you beg for mercy.

59. Turning off the World Series final in the seventh inning because he suddenly must make love to you.

60. Frightening you a little with his intensity.

61. Kissing. Kissing your ass. Stroking the cheeks, making circles, alternating gentleness and assertive pressure. Licking the crack, probing gently, perhaps with his very wet finger, to see if you're interested. Deeper if you seem willing, his thumb rubbing the clitoris at the same time, making you hotter.

62. Tying you with silken sashes to the four corners of the bed and torturing you with pleasure.

63. Giving you the erotic fantasy you really want—a stranger (someone he knows is safe) who will make love to you as he instructs him . . . himself as your slave . . . yourself as a slut. This means he knows you very well.

64. Filling your vagina with a necklace of pearls and pulling it out one pearl at a time.
65. His insisting you go out for the evening with him without panties on.
66. Making love to you with your clothes on, tugging the crotch of your panties to one side, and—seeing how wet you are—entering you forcefully.
67. Ripping your panties off and making love to you standing up.
68. Bringing you a seashell from his walk on the beach and writing inside it "I love you," with his name.
69. Proposing marriage. So old-fashioned. So highly erotic.

69 Ways
to Turn Him On

1. Kissing. Soft lips. Romantic kissing.
2. A compliment. Something extravagant that you really mean.
3. Kissing. Kissing the corners of his mouth. Teasing bites. Invasive kisses.
4. Closing your lips. Not letting his tongue into your mouth. Then suddenly sucking his lower lip, biting it gently.
5. Letting him persuade you even when you've already decided yes.
6. Loving his smells. The sun on his skin. His after-shave smell. His after-six-sets-of-tennis smell. Your obvious delight in all his smells.
7. Kissing. Kissing his fingers. His palm. Licking his palm. Sucking his fingers. Licking between each finger.
8. Letting him undress you. Resisting a little. Resisting a lot. Letting him rip your panties off.
9. Undressing him slowly and making love to each part as it appears.
10. Tearing his shirt off . . . shredding his underwear.
11. Slow dancing naked to the stereo.
12. Treating him to a long lovingly erotic massage with almond oil.

13. Sending him flowers because he will love the smell of freesias.
14. Telling him in a poem how wonderful it was last night.
15. Saying you'd rather have supper in bed tonight and watch a new porn film. Then reenacting the best parts of the movie.
16. Asking him to look at *Penthouse* or *Playboy* with you and tell you which are his favorite breasts and vulvae.
17. Asking him to masturbate while you lick his balls.
18. Confessing to him that you're so hot, you can't wait till you get home and want to go to the nearest motel. Or drive-in movie.
19. Bringing lunch in a basket and a bottle of champagne to his office and locking the door.
20. Pushing him into a closet and rubbing up against him hard.
21. Pinching his rump in public, knowing no one can see.
22. Flirting with him as if you haven't been married for years.
23. Staring at him. Then smiling.
24. Bumping into him.
25. Drawing a perfumed bubble bath for him and washing him all over, paying special attention to his beautiful penis.
26. Buying him a rubber duckie for the bathtub.
27. Grabbing him by the tie and saying "I can't wait."
28. Stroking him with pressure, more pressure than you'd like because that's what he likes.
29. Kissing him roughly. Throwing him onto the bed or the floor and unzipping his pants.
30. Challenging him to wrestle.
31. Telling him what to do to you in bed . . . in the taxi on the way home.
32. Kissing. Kissing his neck and his earlobes. Kissing his eyelids. Kissing the hollows and the bones. Biting his earlobe gently. Sticking your tongue in his ear, just a little, just for a second, to see if he likes it.
33. Rubbing against his body as you dance. Pressing your breasts into him with the most casual kiss.
34. Holding his hands over his head as you ride his penis so that he can feel he's your prisoner.
35. Kissing. Kissing his nipples. Caressing the muscles there with pressure. Flicking the nipple with your finger. With your tongue. Biting it gently. Pinching it hard once he's let you know how hot that makes him.

36. Nibbling. Licking. Sucking. Less-than-serious biting.
37. Sharing your bath or shower. Going down on him in the tub. Teasing his balls with his rubber duckie. Drying him with the towel.
38. Kissing his stomach. Kissing his inner thighs and stroking close to the pubic area without quite touching, using some pressure. Kissing behind his knees.
39. Kissing the bottoms of his feet. Massaging his feet and ankles. Sucking his toes.
40. Sitting on his face.
41. Loving it.
42. Letting yourself come. A lot.
43. Eating him while he's eating you even if it's not your favorite thing because it distracts you from your pleasure. Because *he* likes it.
44. Sucking your thumb while he's thrusting inside you and imagining it's his penis.
45. Asking him to sit on the chair or on the edge of the bed naked so you can kneel between his legs and go down on him.
46. Tying his hands and feet to the bedposts with sashes and belts to torture him with pleasure.
47. Making him try on your underwear.
48. Telling him you love his hands . . . or eyes . . . or mouth . . . or rump . . . whatever is true. These are not clever lines to use. They are how to express what you really feel.
49. Taking off your shoe and tickling his crotch with your toes under the table at dinner. (Only if there's a tablecloth.)
50. Leading him around on a leash. If he can get into it.
51. Being verbal about your pleasure. Making sounds. Telling him it's not just sex . . . it's him.
52. Coming to bed in boots and a lacy garter belt.
53. Asking him to lick your boot.
54. Taking your panties off in the cab and sticking them in his pocket.
55. Getting him to stand in front of a mirror while you kneel and go down on him.
56. Telling him over the phone what you are fantasizing doing to him and what telling him is doing to you. And what you are

wearing . . . very little, sheer and silky . . . and where your fingers are as you talk.

57. Letting him know when he does something wonderful. Perhaps in writing. Sharing with him some new feeling, a sexual high or a first you've reached with him. If it's true.

58. Kissing. Kissing his backside. Stroking the cheeks, making circles, alternating tickling touches and assertive pressure. Licking the crack, sticking your tongue inside, probing with your tongue and your very wet finger. Just a little, to see if he's interested. Deeper if he seems willing. And more. (See pages 130–132.)

59. Hugging him a lot . . . languorous skin-to-skin hugging in bed, hugging him close after sex. Hugging anywhere, anytime, when you just can't keep your hands off him. Don't.

60. If you're always amazed how handsome he is . . . tell him.

61. Shoving him into a dark doorway. Feeling him up. Necking in the car. Making love to him in movie theaters, elevators, on the Staten Island Ferry, during intermission at the ballet, in the stairwell at The Museum of Modern Art, hugging him and petting while waiting for your number to come up at the smoked salmon counter in Zabar's.

62. As you dress for a party, tying a long silk ribbon around his penis, asking him to drape the end over his belt so you can tug on it all night if you feel like it and he won't forget who's the Mistress.

63. Telling him he's a beautiful woman and it's your penis and you're inside him. Use the f word.

64. Doing exactly what he likes to his balls. Licking. Sucking. Gentle tugging. Taking first one and then the other or both into your mouth. Cupping them tightly in your hand as you eat him. Holding them as he comes.

65. Letting him come really fast.

66. Letting him come in your mouth. Enjoying the taste.

67. Telling him everything you think is wondrous about him. What you've heard. What you've discovered. If he's the best—at anything—say so.

68. Looking at him from time to time as you kiss him . . . as you eat him.

69. Surprising him again and again with your sexual response . . . your erotic intensity.

Communication— Getting to Know You in Bed

If only it were as easy to say what you like and want in bed as it is in a restaurant or watching TV. "This fish stinks." "The mashed potatoes taste like library paste." "I'd like my steak very rare but not blue." "This is the stupidest show I've ever watched." "I hate Robert Redford in that movie." "I don't think I can take cartoons before noon, please, baby."

Imagine if you did that in bed. "I want twelve minutes of cunnilingus and then once over lightly." "Who taught you how to kiss?" "There's no way I can go down on you before breakfast."

Talking about what you need or want—where your mate's technique is distracting or turning you off, when you seem to be picking up mixed messages from him and are frustrated at not being able to please—is a delicate art. It's even more difficult when your physical intimacy is brand-new. Even communicating pleasure and delight is difficult for some women. You aren't really sure how experienced he is, or how fragile. You are worried about exposing yourself too much, too soon . . . concerned that he might feel threatened by your need, might find you more sexually sophisticated, even more responsive, than he can handle comfortably.

Try speaking without words if words seem difficult. Touch yourself where you like to be touched, the way you like to be touched. Touch him the way you want him to touch you. If he has his fingers on your clitoris exactly where you want them (good for him, he got there all on his own), you might touch his nipple making the movements you would like him to mimic on your clitoris. He may miss the point: "Playing with my nipples does nothing for me." You can say, "Oh, if you did that to me, I'd be in heaven. And when you touch me like that where your hand is now, I get so hot." If his fingers seem lost, probing inside perhaps when you wish they were exploring an external hot spot, don't snatch them away. Give him some time, then guide them gently. Give him a sense of how much pressure you like with your own fingers, on top of his, pressing.

If he's found your favorite erogenous zone or introduced you to one you didn't know you possessed—got right into your surefire rhythm and set off earth tremors—don't just lie there in frozen animation. Let him know. Murmurs and sighs, a growl . . . whatever comes out, even a scream. The easiest words to say when you're flying are "yes . . . yes!" "It's so good" is a wonderful compliment, especially coming from you when you're clearly barely able to speak. "It's you" sounds ambiguous, but when you open your eyes and smile at him, he'll get the message: it's not just his masterly technique that excites you, it's specifically . . . him.

To Inspire	To Deflate
I love when you kiss my breasts and squeeze them, but it's hottest when you're gentle.	Do you think those are footballs you're playing with?
I love when you tease me and kiss me everywhere with my clothes on.	You're in too big a rush, you lout. I don't think you really like sex.
It's that wild sense of your just barely touching that makes me so hot, not the pressure. That can be too intense. I'm so sensitive right there.	It's a clit, dear, not a gearshift.

To Inspire	To Deflate
It makes mc so hot when you kiss me the way you just did . . . all around my clitoris.	Don't stop. You act as if I taste bad.
Oh baby, that felt so wonderful. I feel tingly all over, and if you touch me like this I know I can come again.	You don't plan to leave me hanging here unsatisfied while you zonk off to sleep, I hope.
Would it excite you to make me come again and again till I can scarcely stand the ecstasy of it? Put your fingers here, and I'll show you.	I think you're jealous because you can't have multiple orgasms. Once, and you're as lively as a beached flounder.
My pussy is on fire . . . you've made it so happy. I think I need to just simmer quietly a little while.	Stop already. You must think I'm a sex machine.
I feel like necking and petting . . . make your lips soft for me. May we pretend we're teenagers?	Why don't you ever kiss me anymore?
If you touch my ass and move your fingers like this, it makes me feel so melting and good.	I'm sick of the same old stuff all the time.
Is this the way Cheryl Tiegs does it in your fantasies, darling?	Stop waving that scarlet rod at me as if it were God's gift to women. I can't figure out what the hell you want me to do.
Tell me, baby, tell me what you want . . . tell me where to put it, may I sit on it now?	I have to stop because I know I'm doing this all wrong.

To Inspire	To Deflate
Stop. Stop. *Stop.* My back just went out. (In emergencies, you don't have to be polite.)	Stop. Stop. *Stop.* My back just went out. (If you're in pain and he thinks you're kidding, it's okay to punch him.)

Serious sexual problems should never be thrashed out at bedtime. Find some relaxed, neutral moment, perhaps when you're both feeling calm and loving and there's no phone or children to interrupt. If necessary, make an appointment for drinks after work or a date for a walk in the park. Avoid the accusatory "you" and tell him how you feel. "I feel lonely when . . ." "I feel abandoned if . . ." "I feel happiest when . . ." "I wonder sometimes if I have . . ." "Am I missing some message?" "We used to have such wonderful . . ." "I've been reading this bawdy, naughty, utterly serious little book, and I wish you would read it too."

USEFUL PHRASES FOR BEGINNERS AND BEGINNINGS

Do Say	Don't Say
Show me.	I have a headache.
I love that.	I think I'm getting my period.
Here.	Should I answer the phone?
Hmmm.	You idiot, that's disgusting.
It's so good.	Why did it get small like that?
Now.	Yecch. Take a shower.
Yes.	Do you always have to be on top?
Yes. Yes. Yes.	You aren't even close.
Look at me.	No.
You're beautiful.	It's spelled c-l-i-t-o-r-i-s.
How did you know.	I give up.
Yes, there.	This is ridiculous.
That's right.	Are you sure that's going to fit?

Do Say	Don't Say

It's so beautiful.

I have to lick this.

Isn't it awfully big?

You just fit.

You fill me up.

It's so hard.

You feel like silk.

I love your ass.

My mouth was made for . . .
you . . . this . . . it.

I love your mouth.

Give me your mouth.

Don't stop.

The answering service will pick
up.

You smell wonderful.

I love how you taste.

Again? So soon.

You amaze me.

I can't believe how wonderful you
are.

Give it to me.

Yes.

I can't believe I'm coming again.

You know everything.

I love the way you are.

Yes. Yes. Yes.

All right. Show me!

I'll swallow it next time.

Was that it?

I mean . . . already?

You're the only one that can't
seem to find it.

I'm sorry. I guess I fell asleep.

Where were we?

Do you hate my stretch marks?

Don't kiss me. I haven't brushed.

That's great but try it two inches
to the left.

Does it always get soft in the
middle like that?

Of course I came. Just because I
don't sing the "Star-Spangled
Banner" doesn't mean I'm not
happy.

You're really odd.

21 Thoughtful and Amusing Things to Do with a Penis

1. Kiss it.
2. Caress it.
3. Lick it.
4. Suck it.
5. Whip it with your hair (be sure you have removed your hot rollers).
6. Rub it against your lips and slap your cheeks with it.
7. Alternately lick it, pinch it gently with your lips, blow on it.
8. Encircle the tip, under the ridge (if there is one), and tug up gently.
9. Admire it profusely.
10. Show that you saw *Deep Throat* too.
11. Hug it between your breasts.
12. Sit on it.
13. Write a poem to it.
14. Once it's wet and sticky, rub it all over your face.
15. Sing to it while licking and kissing. Watch him watching you.
16. Tease it just a little with your teeth.
17. Stroke it, all wet and sticky, while you play with his balls, lick-

ing them and swallowing one at a time, then holding them so they feel cozy.

18. Dip it in peanut butter and lick it off . . . or chocolate sauce . . . or . . .
19. Make it come with your mouth.
20. Savor his come and make happy sounds.
21. Pat it approvingly, kiss it, and say thank you.

How to Find Out What He Really Likes

You need to know the fine details of what pleases him. What does he especially like? Teasing teeth? No teeth ever? Pressure here or there? Long tight strokes of his penis with your hand or loose barely touching ones or both . . . in a very definite order? Does he want sucking or slurping, no loud noises please, talk dirty to me, silence, play with the tip, don't touch it at all, yes, balls . . . no, balls, licks but not . . . the endless subtle variations? How to bring him over the edge faster . . . how to slow and cool him without turning him off . . . how to sense when he's not hot enough to brave the experiment he won't like if he's not super-hot. If he loves to make love, if he's a healthy, open sexual being, he will have no problem letting you know what pleases him.

A grunt, a sigh, a murmur, the expression on his face will tell you. His hand will move your hand. Or he may instruct you, sweetly, even forcefully in an erotic game, rewarding your skill, punishing your miscomprehension with a tone of voice or gesture that will excite you both. Watch how he plays with himself and learn. Let him put your mouth where he wants it. Feel him grow harder and bigger. Look at his eyes. Soon you'll know his arousal pattern as well as you know your neighborhood.

There are likely to be other secrets to pleasing him, secret desires that are not always easy to tell. With time and trust, the two of you can share your unspoken fantasies. In the muted light after lovemaking on a lazy afternoon, you can tell him how wonderful it is to be a woman, what it feels like when he's inside you, how he surprises you as a lover, and the images that flash into your head when you're loving. In this mellow, unguarded moment you both may feel trusting enough to share your deepest sexual desires.

Still he may hesitate. Perhaps he fears he may insult or offend you. Perhaps he is concerned, worried that acting out his secret fantasies may make conventional sex less arousing, or may unleash latent sado-masochistic or homosexual feelings. He may nurse a deep-seated fear that were he to let go at all, he might never regain control of his sexuality. Perhaps he has longings you pretend not to recognize because of your own fears and aversions. You simply do not want to swallow come. You are sure you'll feel like an idiot making love in patent leather boots and a garter belt. You hate that messy feeling of smearing semen over your breasts and stomach. Deep throat is an art you simply cannot master. The idea of sharing him with another woman is terrifying even if you get to enlist the woman. And you'd rather scrub floors and wash windows than be seen naked making love to him with your best friends watching in the next bed. Sorting through your own reactions to know which are rigid and misguided, which are cosmic and final, is an exercise for you to work on.

But let's suppose he's shy or hypersensitive about offending you and he just hasn't found the gentlest way to tell you that he likes to be licked and sucked for twenty minutes before vaginal intercourse or he wants you to penetrate his anus with your finger or let him put your worn panties in his pocket so he can touch them all day.

Today is the day to discover what he wants. Play gin rummy or poker or Pac-Man or pinball for domination points. The winner gets so many minutes of sexual slavery from the loser. If you win, you can satisfy some secret longing you've been hiding and then use your extra points to command him to take over.

Play "Make a Deal." Say "I'll do anything you wish for half an hour tonight, if you'll do so-and-so to me." To make it even easier, here is a page of coupons and barter chits, each good for a sexual treat. Fill in the empty coupon. Make more of your own. If you're still not quite sure of the details, ask for a written scenario. It could be something deliciously bizarre or ridiculous. But how can you know for sure till you try?

BARTER CHITS AND
FANTASY COUPONS

WITH THIS CHIT YOU
CAN PICK ME UP IN
A TAXI AND TAKE ME
TO A MOTEL AND I
WILL BE NAKED
INSIDE MY
RAINCOAT.

THIS COUPON
ENTITLES
BEARER TO
BREAKFAST IN
BED, BASKETBALL
ON TV, AND ME.
SIGNED

HOLDER OF THIS
CARD CAN NAME
THE PLACE AND
STYLE OF OUR
NEXT SEXUAL
ENCOUNTER.

COUPON GOOD
FOR ONE-HALF
HOUR OF
CUNNILINGUS

Ticket entitles bearer to one hour of total passivity next time we make love.

This chit is good for one sublime MASSAGE.

IF YOU HAVE YOUR HANDS ON THIS CHIT, YOU ARE A NAUGHTY BRAT AND I WILL PUNISH YOU.

COUPON FOR FULFILLMENT OF 1 FANTASY. YOU NAME IT.

CHAMPAGNE, STRAWBERRIES, HOMEMADE COOKIES AND A HOT NEW PORN FILM ON TAPE COME WITH THIS COUPON.

I WILL BE YOUR TOTAL SLAVE ALL NIGHT. SIGNED

CAVIAR WITH SOUR CREAM AND ANYTHING ELSE YOU DESIRE: YOUR BED OR MINE.

A ticket for a weekend that will be hotter than our honeymoon and twice as romantic.

Bearer entitled to be tied to
the bedposts and made love
to until he/she begs
for mercy.

THIS IS A
ROUND-TRIP
TICKET TO GREEK

Surprise Me.

POOPSIE...
YOU CAN BE
MAMA'S DARLING
LITTLE BABY
TILL DAWN.
SIGNED... MOM.

THIS CARD IS
PASSAGE AROUND-
THE-WORLD

The Joy of Passivity

Permission to be completely passive is a very special gift. Especially today, when so many of us who care about giving and sharing pleasure have been tutored and inspired in the fine art of making love and pleasing a partner. One glorious byproduct of feminist candor and complaint is that most men have learned a lot about loving women and eagerly accept the idea of lingering foreplay and mutual orgasm. They know there's a clitoris there somewhere, even if they can't always find it. So it's not unlikely that the man in your bed often gets so caught up in numbing you with pleasure that he doesn't leave room for reciprocity. If you're lucky, he is one of those men who will devote endless time to exploring your body and firing your ecstasy. From time to time he may truly not wish you to move—except in animal response to his lovemaking. He wants to do everything. His gratification is to be the instrument of your unsurpassed erotic response, your dizzying explosions, your sublime satiety. The moment when your skin is raw and you lie exposed and vulnerable, stunned and on fire, is his pleasure.

But to give this gift to a man is rarer. Even today, with everyone's gender consciousness raised and so many role reversals common, it isn't easy to persuade even the not-so-macho man to abandon his obligation to reciprocate.

Persuade him. Permission to be totally passive is one of the most thrilling gifts you can give him.

"Just this once," you begin. "Promise me. Don't move. Don't do anything. Let me do everything to you."

Then do it. All the tender, teasing, loving soft kisses. The little nips and licks. The wet kisses. All the caresses that he loves. The strokes of pressure and softness. The firm, strong, aggressive holding and kneading that he needs. Kisses in all his secret places. Skin against skin. Kissing him with your breath and your breasts, your eyelashes and your hair. Doing all the wonderful things to his penis that you know he loves, bringing him to the brink of climax again and again. Then, soaking wet yourself, you climb onto his penis, moving against its hardness. By instinct and habit he will start to thrust.

"Don't move," you will say. "Let me." And you will perhaps even hold his hands down as if he were your prisoner . . . let him feel the erotic thrill of submission as you move in the ways that make him hotter, adjusting your position, not letting him stir—saying *"I* want to fuck *you"*—building his excitement as well as your own to a rhythm where you know he will come.

If you are the sexual creature you want to be—that this book may be helping you be—you will already have had an orgasm or two or six yourself, and now you want him to come, not to hold back sensitively and dutifully as he often does, but to let go—to climax when he wants to, his thoughts blacked out by the intensity of sexual feeling . . . out of control, out of touch, out of his mind. Incredibly moved. Exquisitely shattered.

Because of you.

He Doesn't Like Sex— No Kidding

What an irony. Of course you feel betrayed. He loves you but he doesn't love sex. You—the great sensualist, the sorceress of the bedroom, multiply-orgasmic you (after absorbing the lessons of this sexual primer)—are in love with a man who really doesn't like sex. You've been subtle and direct, sweet and sulky, irresistibly passive and delicately aggressive, playful, delicious, tender, naughty, and neat. What more could contemporary man ask for? What are the symptoms?

He falls asleep in the middle of fellatio.

You show him a sexy passage in the novel you're reading and he switches on a rerun of last month's football game.

You slip into a scarlet silk peignoir and bring him a crystal flute of bubbling champagne. He asks for an Alka-Seltzer.

You reach over to kiss him good night and he's already asleep.

When you try to caress his morning erection, he grabs it away and escapes to a cold shower.

He won't look at pretty girls in *Penthouse.*

He's too tired, too full, too sloshed, too stoned, too busy, too anxious, too broke. Bowling is more fun. He wants to Turtlewax the car now. His back aches. His head aches. His tennis elbow is back. He thinks he has whiplash.

"Didn't we just a few nights ago?" he asks.

"Two and a half weeks."

"Oh."

It's not your imagination. You tried tactful discussion. The two of you have spent six months with a family counselor, and you even tried sex therapy. He dozed off during nonsexual pleasuring and flunked mutual masturbation.

If he will not and cannot adjust, can you? Do you love him and your life enough to accept his definition of sexual contentment, with your fantasies, your fingers, and your vibrator to ease the pangs of deprivation? Unless you find a passion to cool your simmering libido, there will be many nights debating the merits of staying against separation and starting over again on your own. A good therapist can help you make that decision.

Let Your Fingers
Do the Talking

In the kindergarten of sex when the two of you were petting, your fingers probably dared explore anatomy your mouth hesitated to touch at first. And his hands roaming over you—most likely fully clothed—daring to inch up your thigh or press hungrily into a virgin crevice of panty, wrinkling your best pleated plaid skirt, created a rush you will never forget. Perhaps that's why the movie *Body Heat* with Kathleen Turner and William Hurt is hotter than most porn flicks and necking in the back seat of a taxi still makes your blood race.

And fingers—his and yours—extend the sensations of your mouths loving orally, providing pressure and caresses, penetration and tweaking. But fingers alone can fashion arousal, exquisite pleasure, and orgasm. Fingers can be even more specific and subtle than mouths—they get to feel strange and wonderful textures and anatomical landmarks as they dispense ecstasy. And with his hand between your legs, rather than his head, his mouth can find your mouth or breast, his teeth can run sideways across your nipple, and he can watch you trembling and arching with pleasure. For some women direct stimulation to the clitoris should begin gently and increase in pressure and intensity. The same rough handling that may thrill one woman may be unendurable to another. And some want lubrication—saliva or vaginal secretions make perfect balm—before any fingering.

What makes you hottest when you masturbate is likely to turn you on instantly when he does it. He might try fingers tickling thighs, gently tugging at pubic hairs, tapping gently everywhere in the geographical zip code of the clitoris . . . except the clitoris itself. Try palm pressing the mons veneris, palm cupping the entire vaginal area, thumb just brushing the clitoral hood. Try pulling the lips back, opening them, exploring the inner lips, tapping the clitoris very lightly, tapping it harder . . . tweaking it with a lubricated finger. Try two or three fingers inside, moving . . . undulating, pressing hard against the top of vagina—the sweet spot, the G-spot—thumb still caressing the clitoris with an intensity and touch that seem to be pleasing you. He might want to press a finger against your anus, too, even push it inside if he sees that you respond to that. Or he can kiss and bite your buttocks as his fingers make their magic. He can pull you close, hugging you to him, your bottom tucked against his front to give a sense of domination as the intensity mounts—you wiggle in excitement but can't get away. Best of all, he knows the subtle intricacies of a woman's climax. He doesn't stop when he feels you begin to arch and throb. He goes on and on and on, beyond your coming, letting you come again if you wish, not stopping till moans and screams and fantasy "no's" become real and you pull away—burning, flesh raw as if the skin is seared away.

How do men feel discovering that a finger on the clitoris can be more powerful magic than the almighty penis thrusting inside? Some are bewildered and not really sure exactly what technique pleases. A man may be shattered to learn that a lot of orgasms he remembers may have been faked by a loving woman wanting not to hurt or disappoint. And the idea that a woman can climax easily with or without his participation may disturb him for a while. But men who like women and the man who loves you will most likely soon discover the thrill of new ways to give you pleasure. One man told Shere Hite that after he learned how to bring his wife to climax with his hand, "I fell in love with her all over again. She was *much* more interested in sex than before. It was bliss."

If your man doesn't already know bliss, it's your pleasant exercise for the day to show him.

The Message
Is Massage

The massage that soothes . . . the massage that energizes . . . the massage that arouses. Massage is an art. Learning to play skin, muscle, nerve, and erotic connections is so much easier than learning to play the violin and, unless you play like Isaac Stern, infinitely more seductive.

When he is weary from a long commute home, tense and drained from the demands of a workday, languorous foreplay and hot playful sex are probably the last thing your man has in mind. But after a relaxing hot soak in a tub frosted with sea salt and a long, loving, relaxing massage by you, he may be restored to healthy animal vigor. And as your strokes become more teasing, as your fingers brush his anatomical hot spots, you may find that what walked in the door, an indifferent mass of tense protoplasm, is transformed into a hungry lover.

If the two of you are new to all this, he may be shy or self-conscious or doubtful. But can anyone resist a really good back rub? Stand behind his chair and knead his neck and upper back; stretch with your thumb and press with the knuckles. Once he's captured by the luxury of your soothing hands, he may be ready for the extended ritual.

Lock the bedroom door. Soften the glare of a small lamp with a rose-colored throw, or light a candle. Take the phone off the hook. If he's too tired or cranky for a hot bath or shower, get him to undress and lie face down on the bed. You have almond oil or baby oil or something unscented in the same bedside basket that holds your vibrator and favorite erotic literature and girly magazines. Warm the oil under hot water or in your hands before you begin. Is baby oil a false message? Too perfumed with nostalgia? For a few minutes perhaps he may feel like an adored pampered baby, but soon he will feel sensual adagios more provocative than Mama's.

His eyes are already closed, so he can't see that you are naked under your robe, which you now set aside—so your body can absorb the oil too—as you straddle his back and begin again. First oiling an expanse of skin, then stretching and kneading, pulling up on shoulders, letting them drop, concentrating on neck and clavicles, working away the knots, smoothing, stroking, and kneading the upper arms, vigorously, firmly, with pressure. Now settle yourself below his rump and concentrate on his back, pressing down and upward with both hands (a little like giving artificial respiration), adding the weight of your body to give a real stretch. Lift the flesh along the ribs and smooth it back. Lean forward, brushing your breasts against his back. Press your fingers into each crevice of his spine, moving upward to the neck. Then do the back again, deep, long, weighted strokes.

Warming and smoothing oil on as you go, settle to one side and, letting one arm fall loosely, take his other hand. Massage the palm with the heel of your hands, press the hand between yours, then work all the bones and flesh of each finger between your thumb and forefinger— from the littlest finger to the thumb, pressing, pinching, stretching. Now, starting at the wrist, work up the arm, kneading and stretching, biceps and triceps and under the arm, too. Then hold his hand with one hand, encircle the wrist with your other hand, and move it up, stretching and pulling the whole arm. Repeat on the other side. Give the same attention to feet and toes—perhaps even more, hard with your palm and knuckles. Feet have strange and wonderful connections to erogenous sensors. Massage each toe, pinching and pulling from the foot to the tip of the nail. Knead the calves and knees and thighs, then stretch and stroke with knuckles and fingers—just brushing the scrotum as you go up, as if by accident.

Now you focus on his wonderful tail assembly. Circle the buttocks, kneading and pressing especially where the thigh ends and his buttocks begin. Just by the way you drizzle the oil and concentrate on his bottom, adding feathery little strokes and perhaps brushing it with your breasts, you signal your own growing excitement. Working on the body you love, hearing his moans and sighs of pleasure, perhaps rubbing your clitoris against his heel or on your own, has you quite turned on.

Don't even ask him to turn. Let him be totally lost in sensual pleasure, too blissed out to move. Tug him over. If his penis is pointing into the air or halfway there (although it may not be), you can pretend to ignore it. Instead, straddle his chest, working on his neck and shoulders again, his upper arms, then moving downward on his torso, tending to his chest and stomach. You may even turn your bottom to his face so you can knead and stroke his legs again, ignoring his erection . . . concentrating on the thighs, most especially the inner thighs, your caresses growing more and more erotic, your fingers moving up the leg just brushing his genitals.

If midway he hasn't grabbed you and insisted you sit on his penis, or thrown you to the bed to mount you, or thrust into you from behind . . . if he's still purring and sighing and touching himself as he grows hard . . . you might dribble a few drops of oil on his penis, massaging it gently at first and then more firmly and then very lovingly and then with your mouth.

At this moment you have every reason to feel he owes you an equally sublime massage, but don't even consider it. Take advantage of his heat. Sit on his penis and ride yourself to as many orgasms as you desire and deserve. You can have your massage next time. If he's never had a massage quite so wonderful before, all he knows is what he's learned from you. And you can show him more . . . how to stroke your breasts very gently, what kind of touch and pressure you prefer. And if he's as sensual as you are, he'll come up with erotic surprises all his own . . . like spilling wildly slippery love potion over your clitoris into the lips of your vagina, the warmth and perfume of the oil and his fingers everywhere building a frenzy of pleasure, a prelude to wonderfully slithery sex.

By the way, giving or getting a sense-dizzying, muscle-melting massage is not a legally binding contract. A lightning transition to heated vaginal intercourse is not guaranteed. No matter how erotic it is for you, it may be soporific for him—or vice versa. But if you've mastered the art, the massage was certainly both sensual and sexual, for the kneader and the needy, who could both wake a bit early tomorrow, hungry for love.

Eat to Win—
Fellatio

Men love to be eaten. In a lifetime of sexual adventure you are more likely to meet he-men who hate football and racy sports cars and love quiche than you are to find a man who hates fellatio. Oh, I'm sure they exist. I myself have yet to meet one. Many men rank oral sex as the most intimate sexual act. They long for it when they don't have enough. First of all, fellatio just simply feels wonderful. And symbolically it's seenas your affection if not admiration for an aspect of his anatomy he is wildly fond of.

How do you feel about fellatio? Be honest. Are you ambivalent? Share your doubts.

"I don't want to . . . because he'll think I'm too experienced."

Answer: Tell him you've hardly ever done it before but you were inspired by the beauty of his penis.

"I don't want to . . . because it's disgusting and dirty."

You have more bacteria in your mouth. Will you give up kissing? Dab some whipped cream on his penis and lick it off. You may get caught up in the culinary experience and forget your aversion.

"I'm a feminist and I won't get on my knees to service a man."

Put your head on some pillows and make him get on his knees in front of you. There are many fantasies about giving head—some are fantasies of submission, some unleash feelings of power and control.

"I read fellatio is illegal and perverse, and wasn't that what they were doing in Sodom and Gomorrah?"

Smoking grass is illegal too, and driving without a seat belt, and whose husband was it that you were sleeping with last summer while his wife was at the beach with the kiddies?

"I don't want to . . . because it's fattening. I'm on a very strict diet."

You aren't required by contract to swallow all his come, or even a little, and anyway, sperm, even a generous serving of it, has fewer calories than plain low-fat yogurt.

"I don't want to . . . because it smells funny."

If he has washed, it probably has no smell at all. Take a shower together and have your first orgasm in the bathtub and forget about odors.

"I'm afraid I'll gag."

Try licking it first. Pretend it's an ice cream cone. Use your hand in conjunction with your mouth. Practice on a banana. Bananas are rich in potassium. A penis is rich in appreciation.

"He can't stop nagging me about this."

I thought you wanted to please him.

"I would be perfectly happy to go down on him if he weren't so stubbornly opposed to going down on me."

I don't blame you for being annoyed. But blackmail and threats and punishing him can't be as effective as negotiation in a nonsexual setting. Exchange some barter chits (see pages 97–99). Perhaps he isn't sure how to please you? (Let him read "Good Enough to Eat—Cunnilingus," pages 115–117.) Once he sees how much pleasure he can give you, he may discover that he likes it.

Are you still ambivalent about fellatio? Perhaps you hesitate because you just aren't sure what to do. You go along with pleasing him orally because you love him and you don't want to lose him—or because how can you refuse if you want to be considered a good lover? There are women who love giving head and actually climax from the excitement. A virtuoso of fellatio has discovered a powerful form of self-expression, plus a surefire way to get more and better sex. This is a woman talking who loves to go down on her man:

I love to do it. He knows how much I love it. That excites him even more. I love to be able to turn a man on—to see that stunned ecstasy on his face, to know that I was the one who did it. At that moment I feel he is giving himself to me. That I am seeing him at his most vulnerable. I take my time . . . I don't always have endless time to devote, but when I do, I take his penis in my hand as if it were the miracle it is—as if it were the object of devotion, and with me it is. I might start out just licking the tip, then licking it all around, circling the rim with my tongue, teasingly at first, then unexpectedly taking the whole shaft into my mouth, relaxing the back of my throat so even a really big penis slips in.

Then I might tease it some more with slurping licks, as if it were a lollipop, apply suction, taking most of it inside my mouth and running my tongue up and down and around, then two or three deep strokes where my lips might land on his balls, which I hold bunched upward in one hand. Then, when he's wet all over, I might just hold his penis in one hand, stroking it, while I lick or poke his balls with my tongue or take first one and then the other into my mouth.

I suck again, long strokes, and then pull the skin down as far as it goes with my hand and lick him all over again, or encircle the ridge with my thumb and forefinger and pull up, squeezing the tip a little . . . if he likes it, if he can take it. Every man is different.

Sometimes I crouch between his legs like a cat. And sometimes I lie stretched out beside him—my vagina near his mouth so he can play with my clitoris. And sometimes I sit on his knee and make myself wetter rubbing against the bone—I can come that way, and sometimes I do, holding his penis in my hand and stroking till the orgasm subsides. My saliva seems to grow thicker the hotter I get and the more wildly I am eating him, the wetter he is—and now I'm giving him the pressure and rhythm I know that he wants (because I experimented and watched or asked or he told me), and knowing how close he is, I can get wilder, with every stroke, the back of my throat relaxed and open.

And when he begs me to climb onto his penis because he's so close to coming, sometimes I do. But often I'll say, "No, I want you to come in my mouth." And I may or may not swallow most of it, but I love the smell and usually I like the taste, and I like the feel of it sticky and warm on my face, in my hair, on the bed. I feel very animal. I love that feeling. When we've gone on like that for a long time, I might collapse too, but sometimes I will suck him once or twice just after he comes. Not all men will permit it. But some find the torture exquisite. And I tell him how wonderful he tastes. And if he likes it, I may take everything, his spent penis and balls, and cozy them in one hand while we nap or sleep or talk in that wonderful closeness after sex.

Some men want just to be encircled with the mouth, no pressure. But most want your mouth and hand together to grip like a wet, hot little vagina.

"If a man wants aggressive oral sex—literally to fuck my mouth—I can get into that fantasy. (When your lovemaking gives each of you a chance to dominate, submission needn't become a political issue.) If he grabs me by my hair and makes Tarzan noises or slaps his penis against my face, I might be amazed but I'm probably also amused, if I'm not lost in an exciting fantasy of submission." (Since this woman is president of a major publishing company, we don't have to worry that she carries her submissiveness into real life.)

When people call it a blow job, it really sounds like work. And if you are a lukewarm practitioner of fellatio, it may seem like work. But once you get the knack—and discover the thrill of being a world-class fellatrice, plus the pleasure of delivering so much pleasure—you might perceive its erotic impact for you.

Just remember: every penis is different. Every man has his own special quirks and affections, a spot too sensitive to touch or an anatomical detail that needs special devotion. Most men will find you rudely carnivorous if you graze them with teeth, so keep your lips drawn over ivory . . . but know that gentle nips and delicate teasing with teeth can make some men wildly excited. Fellatio combined with anal play may arouse him, too, or simply squeezing his buttocks or pressing on the perineum.

Don't be discouraged by a soft penis in a man who clearly wants to make love. Your hand and mouth can be an instant Erector set. If he's tired or feeling the years or has already come once, it may take longer. If you want to study passionate fellatio solo at your leisure or with a friend, get the porn flick *Tigresses,* a graduate course in oral technique.

An effective chronology for foreplay that is most likely to satisfy a

woman is hugging and kissing and stroking with cunnilingus first, perhaps an orgasm or two for you, then fellatio till he's on the brink, then a
fast transition into sexual intercourse. This is not a recipe. Or a scenario
or scripture . . . just a theme with variations you can improvise on.

Good Enough to Eat— Cunnilingus

By definition, a great lover is a master of cunnilingus. Ultimately, any man who likes women will discover the complex sensual and emotional pleasures of cunnilingus. Some men are poets, celebrating the deliciousness of a woman's body with metaphors and compliments that will stun you—like "golden honeypot." Some men are languorous athletes, thrilled with how easy it is to give you pleasure and even orgasm after orgasm with or without an erection, before or after his own orgasm, exerting virtually no energy at all. Nothing makes a good man hotter than knowing how hot he is making you. So don't just lie there like a limp noodle. Don't be afraid to wiggle and squeal and let your toes curl if you feel like it. Open your mouth and see what sounds emerge. Even a master likes to hear how wonderful he is.

There are men, alas, who rarely initiate cunnilingus. Your man may have his own hangups about kissing a vagina, a real or exaggerated fear of unpleasant odors, an unhappy experience in the past. Or perhaps he's picking up from the way your legs are laced together or how you keep sliding out of his reach that you have doubts.

Imagine the first brave soul who had the courage and creativity to eat an oyster—that squirmy, slimy, briny little bivalve—and his pleased shock at its tangy fragrance and sublime taste. Your natural tang is lovely. Some men will tell you it's a nectar they adore. Don't take my word for it. Kiss his mouth when he's glistening from loving you and see how you taste. Naturally, you don't want to be too tangy. So wash well with soap before you come to bed. The vagina is basically self-cleansing inside a woman who is healthy and free of infection, but you may want to douche with warm water once in a while and very occasionally with vinegar (one tablespoon to a quart of water). If you don't overfill the inside cup of your diaphragm (one teaspoon of jelly is enough), and slip it in carefully, then wash all around (saving the final applicatorful of spermicide till just before intercourse), you are still likely to be delicious. In taste tests by experts, Koromex jelly has been rated acceptably palatable, better than most others. If your pubic hair is soft and downy, you can tuck a small flower or two into it. If it is wild and frizzy, you might want to experiment with clipping it very short. To please yourself. And perhaps please him. Perfume worn by the pulse in the hollows of your knees becomes your aura.

Learning the artistry of cunnilingus is like mastering a foreign language—the tongue becomes a more delicate instrument. And he may never be quite sure how skilled he is. (It's not like a marathon, where your score is posted and you know how far behind the winner you were.) His reluctance to go down on you may be confusion about what you really want and what pleases you. Of course, unless you've been with a wise and practiced lover before, how can you know? "Try anything," you can say. "Try everything. This is all new to me, and I'm sure I'll love it."

He might begin with fingers and kisses, working down your body, paying a courtesy call on each erogenous zone, then licks on the inner thighs moving toward the outer vaginal lips, opening the lips and circling around with his tongue . . . knowing by your sounds and movement what pleases you. It may take actual clitoral contact to ignite your electricity. And too much direct pressure can make some clits numb. You may need ten to fifteen minutes of intense stimulation, a building of rhythm that doesn't break till you dissolve in climax.

Meanwhile, his hands may be squeezing your buttocks or playing with your breasts, or pressing down on the mons veneris. His fingers may be inside you, two or three of them, with a kind of urgent force that is igniting the G-spot. If his mouth wanders and he seems lost, adjust your position till the electricity sparks once again, or guide him with your hands on either side of his head, or pull his hair. Do squirm against his tongue. Pull the mons veneris up to expose the clitoral shaft if that feels good. He's down there between your legs to please you. Once you show him how, you'll never have to debate the wisdom of faking anything again. Your response will make him feel like Superman. If you like to have an orgasm as fast as you can and another one or two before intercourse, he'll be delighted to know it, and if one searing explosion is all you can bear in one evening, he'll indulge you. He may even have an orgasm just from giving cunnilingus. (A man that sexual will become erect again if you're lucky and want to come a second time in some other form of sex play.)

There are true cunnilingus addicts—men for whom nothing is quite so satisfying as going down on you. They can go on endlessly for hours and as many orgasms as you can endure. Who knows what fantasies flash through their delightfully obsessed brains. Taunt him. "Are you my sex slave?" "Are you a naughty puppy licking your mistress?" "Are you a panther with a mean, rough tongue?" "Am I your prisoner?"

He may respond. Perhaps he'll get even hotter if you hold his head with an intimation of force. Or you can feed his fantasy of submission by sitting on his face and demanding that he lick you for hours.

Is it different or better than it's ever been? Tell him. Tell him again.

Overrated 69

In the most unlikely case that you're a dud at the old math, it's called sixty-nine (69) because two bodies devoted to mutual oral lovemaking resemble those numbers, one tucked into the other. If I declare that sixty-nine is wildly overrated, I risk cries of outrage from men and women who think it's the ultimate turn-on.

Decide for yourself. Perhaps the simultaneous doubleheader makes sense as a rewarding variation in sex play. And perhaps you love it. But for some, taking turns in the sixty-nine position works better. Giving pleasure while getting pleasure can be distracting. You long to surrender to your growing arousal but dare not—and cannot—while his penis is in your mouth. You might even bite it if you give in to the ecstasy you feel and forget where you are. Eating and being eaten are both such sublime joys, you want to savor them one at a time. And to reach a climax you may have to abandon pleasuring him as you give in to the rush of intense feeling, then go back with full attention to his climax.

Vaginal Intercourse— Is It Obsolete?

Let's put vaginal intercourse back on its pedestal. I'm not suggesting we jostle the clitoris from its lofty heights. The clitoris has earned its permanent niche in the Sensuality Hall of Fame. But if you agree that sex is not merely vaginal intercourse, but hugging and kissing, caressing and sucking, here, there, and everywhere, with the goal not orgasm but sensual pleasure, I think it's safe to restore cachet to the battered image of vaginal sex—"the divine old in-and-out," as one of my lustier friends likes to put it.

The honorable reputation of vaginal intercourse has suffered mightily in two decades of feminist enlightenment and sexual exploration. When Shere Hite's report on female sexuality documented what many women already knew—that most women do not reach orgasm from simple intercourse—frustrated women and good men went off in search of the elusive clitoris. What stood out from Hite's work was the devastating news that women had their most powerful orgasms from masturbation. What tended to be overlooked was that their most meaningful orgasms were with a man.

The challenge was clear. If we could figure out what made us hot and communicate our secrets to men (without rendering them impotent or hostile), life would be a dream, sweetheart. Interestingly, in her later report on male sexuality Hite found most men knew about the need for clitoral stimulation but believed their women were among the 30 percent who could climax from vaginal thrusting, as a "mature" woman would.

Clearly, certain positions create clitoral friction. Others provide intense stimulation to the G-spot. And some women will climax during thrusting simply because stimulation during foreplay has them so hot they are ripe to explode from almost any further provocation—a slow, probing sensuous kiss, sensitive fingers brushing a nipple, squeezing the breasts, the pressure of a palm on the mons veneris. But many women can climax only from clitoral foreplay. Others need clitoral stimulation during thrusting or afterward or both.

Here are some scenarios for very hot and sublime, if not orgasmic, pleasure.

HER ORGASM IN FOREPLAY

Saturday Night Live, Act I. Their hands meet at the decanter as she reaches to pour for him and he reaches to pour for her. He plays with her palm as they wait for dessert. Her fingers pull the tight curls at the back of his neck. Their thighs press together on the banquette. He has his hand under her skirt. "Why are you so wet?" he asks.

Act II. They dance. The music slows. He pulls her close. She kisses his neck and moves with him, and against him, too. "The cabbie is watching us," she whispers as he unbuckles her garter and bites her thigh. "I don't care," he says. "Show him everything."

Act III. Inside the apartment, they drop their coats, bodies locked. They kiss. She tugs his tie loose. He reaches into her blouse and bares a breast for his kiss. "You must like me an awful lot," she says, unzipping his trousers. "Look how big this is."

"Take off your panties," he says, "or I'll rip them off." He makes love to her with his lips and fingers, there on the floor, on cushions tugged down from the sofa. He wets his thumb inside her and strokes her clitoris till she comes, then more, till she comes again, shuddering. He holds her close . . . her hand wiggles between them and she strokes him, making love to his penis with her mouth, gauging his excitement.

She stops; he takes his penis in his own hand and rubs it against her clitoris, till she comes again. Then he mounts her and moves in the rhythm that pleases him till he climaxes.

HER ORGASM DURING INTERCOURSE

Thunderdome, Act I. He reaches for her breast with one hand and for her clitoris with the other. She gets hot so quickly. She is impatient to have him inside her. "You fill me up," she says. "It's always the same. I can't believe how good it feels." And she likes to take charge, putting herself into the positions that make her hottest, touching herself and then reaching back to hold his balls in her hand, coming close to climax again and again, then stroking herself in the special way she knows will make her come quickly just seconds before he climaxes too.

HER ORGASM AFTER INTERCOURSE

The Long-Distance Runner, Act I. She flirts, kissing his fingers, sharing a glass of champagne, necking in the carport. He wants to undress her and make love in the back seat. "No. In the house," she says. Pouring a glass of Cognac, she takes a swallow in her mouth and takes his penis in too, swirling the Cognac around it.

Act II. She loves what he does to her with his mouth. "Come let's do that in bed," she says, undressing him and herself. She goes down on him. He is rubbing her clitoris with his fingers and he knows she is close to climax. She pulls away, presenting her derrière to him. He enters her from behind and, thrusting hard, quickly comes. He turns her over and presses his hand on her mons, his fingers teasing her clit till she starts to moan and writhe. He holds her tightly, increasing the pressure of his stroke, varying the movement, feeling the tension as she arches and climaxes. "I love that long incredible up-and-down ride," she says. "But

I can only come once. It's so violent and intense, I couldn't possibly do it again."

ASK DR. GAEL

Why am I dry? It could be your cold pill or the grass you smoked before bedtime. Or the fact that you douched just minutes ago. Suppressed anger can turn off the normal flow of lubrication, too. Some therapists think that Kegel exercise helps increase blood flow to the vaginal area, improving natural lubrication. When you feel the need, use saliva, KY jelly, or any sterile water-soluble lubricant. Sex shops sell Slippery Stuff—it's super-slick, as advertised.

He hogs the blankets. What can I do? Snuggle closer to him. If he's a chronic blanket or quilt grabber, he may also be a bed hogger. Get up and slip under the covers on the empty side of the mattress. Keep an extra blanket handy nearby. Blanket hogging is definitely not grounds for divorce.

He snores. Help! Try to get him to turn over into a position where he doesn't snore, gently so as not to wake him. Jostle him half awake, then fall asleep quickly before he starts snoring again. Buy some earplugs.

My man comes too quickly. What can I do? If you don't make love very often or haven't been together for a long while or have been turning each other on teasingly all evening, don't be surprised if your man comes very quickly. A second go-round may be smooth and slow. The two of you can also agree to put long, languorous, intensely exciting, potentially orgasmic foreplay before vaginal intercourse, so his fast climax will be less frustrating for you.

If his too-swift ejaculation is persistent, the two of you may want to try being your own sex therapists. A stop-and-start technique involving stimulation just to the verge of orgasm, then a cooling distraction, may help him learn to better control his responses. To master this and the squeeze technique, consult Masters and Johnson's *Human Sexual Inadequacy.* Or you may decide to consult a sex therapist.

Is it okay to have sex during menstruation? Yes. Wash well, then slip a diaphragm correctly into place, and no one need know you're menstruating.

Is there more to life than a relentless search for ecstasy? Not in my book.

Orgasm— The Power of O

When an Indian woman climaxes she speaks of "perpetual happiness." To the French it is *le petit mort*—the little death. By comparison, our offhand "I'm coming" seems irreverently nonchalant. Let's begin by exploring attitudes toward orgasm.

What is orgasm?

a. A male-chauvinist conspiracy to make you feel inadequate.

b. Fire created by a kind of primitive friction.

c. A notch on his belt to make him feel more masculine.

d. Proof of your love.

e. Temporary insanity.

f. A good reason to turn off the vibrator.

g. An intense sensation at the peak of sexual arousal followed by a release of sexual tension, possibly accompanied by contractions of the pelvic muscles.

h. The earth moves.

i. Intense pleasure followed by release.

j. Researchers don't agree.

k. A lonely feeling because he falls asleep in forty-two seconds.

If you checked **a, c, d,** you do have problems. If he demands an orgasm from you as proof of your love or confirmation of his machismo and you feel less womanly for failing him, you are indeed a victim of a disorganized tyranny. Sex should be about pleasure, not focused totally on orgasm, and a mature, informed, loving, sensitive man should be able to accept that your orgasm most likely comes from clitoral stimulation—his fingers, your own, oral loving, feathers, vibrators, teddy bears, whatever—without a crisis of masculinity. Love does not lead to orgasm, nor does his sexual virtuosity—but through trust and the security of his love you may find or expand your orgasmic potential. Anger and frustration may be unspoken, unrealized factors in your inability to let go sexually.

If you checked **b, e, h,** you're more of a poet than a scientist but your metaphor sounds good to me.

If you checked **f**—perhaps you're developing an adolescent dependency relationship with your vibrator. Yes, I know vibrators never forget Valentine's Day and don't get soft when you're just starting to get warm, and vibrators mean you never have to say you're sorry. Vibrators are a surefire way to orgasm for many women who cannot climax easily any other way, and it can be really hot when he uses the vibrator on you. But it is possible to become addicted to the vibrator, so that mere cunnilingus and masturbation, even your own knowing fingers, no longer can satisfy. You wouldn't want to give up fresh peach or chocolate fudge ice cream just because butterscotch nut swirl is so delicious. Keep your options open.

If you checked **g, i, j,** you're in touch with where most psychologists and sexologists are today. They don't agree. Some believe there is no orgasm without direct clitoral stimulation (though Kinsey suggested that some women can climax from fantasy alone). Others insist there is an area of acute sensitivity (most likely to be found in the front of the vagina) that can trigger vaginal orgasms in some women, even the release of fluid in a few women.

If you checked **k,** know that you are not alone. Even a very loving and romantic man may feel he has given his all and fall deeply asleep seconds after sex. Writing in *Forum,* Dr. C. A. Tripp cites loss of energy —"the male orgasm drains and depletes at least 17 glands, glands that are not ordinarily ready to fire again (nor to support erotic excitement) for half an hour or more"—and the biological implications that link orgasm and death in many lower species—bees, spiders, and certain fish. So if he's off like a flounder, it has nothing to do with you, Dr. Tripp observes. Step back yourself, he advises: "It is likely to greatly shorten his absence."

Missionary
Impossible

Not everyone is as flexible as a pretzel, and perhaps no one will
necessarily want to try every single position for making love documented in the *Kama Sutra*. But if you always find yourself sitting on
top facing Bloomingdale's (the joke says that's the best position to make
a Jewish American Princess come fast), you might like to consider other
choreography that is almost as thrilling. Civilization began with the
woman on top. At least, it seems so in classical Greece and ancient
Rome. Excavations in Mesopotamia dating from 3000 B.C. often show
the female superior, an image that appears everywhere in the art of
early Peru, India, China, and Japan. Then along came Christianity and
everything got turned upside down. To make love in any position more
exotic than the missionary was grounds for a perversity citation. In the
past decade man-on-top has become a political issue, but depending
where your legs are and where your fingers (or his) are and what your
aerobically trained body does while he perches there, missionary need
not be impossible, even though coming on top is often easier.

Since everyone is built differently, a particular coital arrangement
may provide more or less friction, deep or stunningly deep penetration
and clitoral stimulation or none. Where the bones jut or curve, where
too much tummy or a well-endowed rump conspire to keep you two

apart will affect connection and feeling. A man may lack the flexibility to sit on his thighs, a position that makes all kinds of incendiary interlocking possible. If you had any doubts how being in shape can enhance lovemaking, doubt no more.

1. Man on top. Woman with legs clasped around him.
2. Man on top. Woman knees to chest.
3. Man on top. Woman with legs in a wide V, thrusting up.
4. Man sitting on thighs, woman's body pulled toward him.
5. Man sitting on thighs, woman lifting herself up and down on his penis, a pelvic lift. Permits G-spot stimulation.
6. Man kneeling, woman on her back, one leg out, one leg up, in a scissors position. Permits deep penetration.
7. Woman on top, kneeling, moving back and forth. Good clitoral stimulation if anatomies permit.
8. Woman on top, body pressed close to his, man thrusting.
9. Woman on top, legs straight out in front of her, man's hands on her legs, her hands behind her for balance, helping her move back rapidly with the penis pulled totally horizontal. Some men love it.
10. Woman on top, body dropped backward down to his knees (if you do yoga you can do this). This presents an invitation for his hand to indulge her clitoris.
11. Woman on top, squatting, lifting herself up and down on his penis. He may help lift her.
12. Woman on top, backward, facing his feet, sitting and moving up and down.
13. Woman on top, slides down, folding one of his legs so that they are twigging, with his penis inside her. Deep penetration and intense stimulation for him. Woman can move easily.
14. Man on his back. Woman on her back with his penis inside her.
15. Man on top, woman's legs down and straight out. Makes a very tight vagina.
16. Man spooning woman from behind, and just below so that he can slip inside. She can then rotate her body for maximum G-spot stimulation.
17. The X, stretched out, face to face, woman on top, their legs interwoven.
18. Man on top, woman with upper body over the edge of bed, hands on the floor for balance. A double rush.

19. She lies on her back, one leg stretched out, the other knee bent. He lies at right angles to her, one leg under the outstretched leg, the other over the steepled leg. Another scissors position, this one allowing for languorous, no-energy thrusting.

20. Rear entry, doggy style. Woman on hands and knees. A position where testicles may hit the clitoris.

21. Rear entry. Woman on elbows and knees. Deep penetration.

22. Rear entry. Woman flat on her stomach, man kneeling on top. With a strong Kegel-trained muscle, a woman can do wonderful squeezes for both herself and her man in this position.

23. Woman kneeling on edge of bed. Man standing next to bed.

24. Woman standing, bent forward over back of chair or bed. Man standing, entering from behind.

25. Man carrying woman impaled on his penis. Best in a hallway where the walls are close enough to help you both survive.

26. Man on chair. Woman sitting on his lap facing him.

27. Man on chair. Woman on his lap facing away.

28. Woman on a red velvet swing. Man standing.

Legend suggests that there are 101 positions, including woman with foot on man's shoulder standing up . . . but our goal here is quality, not quantity.

Anal Sex— The Ultimate Taboo

Anal sex is very special, linked to secret fantasy and taboo. Some lovers regard sharing the anus as an act of ultimate trust and giving. For others, licking, kissing, fingering, and penetrating a partner's anus fulfills fantasies of submission, domination, even perversion. And they are aroused by the thrill of the forbidden. Physiologically, of course, the nerve endings in the anus are highly sensitive and may add to erotic arousal.

Some women love anal sex. Some women love it sometimes. Some women don't mind it on occasion. But some find it painful or unpleasant or aesthetically disturbing. And some don't care ever to try. Interestingly, a recent survey reports that many younger women enjoy anal sex. You can be a very creative and caring lover and still choose not to have anal sex. Anal penetration is not a particular desire of some men. For others curiosity has led to a trial or two and then indifference. Others might like it occasionally as a sexual variation. But a few men seem to prefer it to all other sex play or expect to enjoy it every time.

Anal sex is considered extremely high-risk in the transmission of AIDS, and till more is known about what makes one person vulnerable to the disease and others seemingly resistant, you will want to use a condom or avoid anal sex altogether except with a longtime mate whom you *know* is and has been truly monogamous.

If the two of you fit into the no-risk category, you may want to explore anal erotica—touching with a finger while playing with yourself or making love. Kissing, licking, penetrating your partner's anus with a finger or a dildo . . . being kissed and licked by him.

Anal sex play need never go beyond mutual stroking, tonguing, kneading of buttocks, licking and kissing of your most private aperture, to be exciting and disinhibiting.

Anal intercourse need not be painful if you go slowly, using plenty of KY jelly or other water-soluble lubricant. Ask him to lick, kiss, and caress your buttocks and anus without penetration so you can enjoy the turn-on without anxiety. If you're feeling lukewarm but still game to experiment, wait for the near-climactic moments of a really hot encounter. Perhaps even after you've come once or twice and he's close to climax too. As he strokes your bottom, licking the crack, pressing his thumb on the clitoris at the same time, let yourself feel the tickle of excitement build. Tensing the anus and then letting go is a way to help the anal muscles relax before he goes deeper. You can learn to control both rings of muscle, and may even climax from thrusting or as he strokes your clitoris. (Remember to wash fingers, penis, or any sex toy before moving from the anus back to the vagina.) If a man urinates soon after anal intercourse, the urine will carry away any organisms that may have slipped into his urethra.

If your longtime mate enjoys anal play, you probably know it. But if you are only now beginning to explore each other, he may be curious enough to try for the first time. When he's really hot, perhaps while you're going down on him, try touching the anus, applying external pressure. Then, with a very wet finger, penetrate just an inch. Stop and wait for the muscles to spasm and then relax. You'll know if he wants you to go further. If he seems to welcome the invasion, put your finger deeper inside, moving it in tiny circles as he thrusts inside you. (See "Understanding His Anatomy," pages 38–40.)

Imagination colors the act. One woman's excitement soars because not being able to see him when he pins her to the bed with his weight intensifies her feeling of not being able to resist. Another imagines her man is riding her as if she were a horse, pulling her head back with her hair as the reins, his thrust driving her to greater and greater ecstasy. A third woman feels that she and her longtime mate have never been closer, their anal experience taking them across a barrier to total intimacy. Another is moved by a sense of wonder and power as her man responds to her penetration of "that secret core." She feels "he has exposed more of himself to me."

Advanced anal sex includes penetration with objects—dildos, vibrators, fists. Some men and women find enemas erotic. And there is even a large two-headed dildo, soft as skin, with fleshlike veins and wrinkles, shaped like a man's penis with a glans at either end. One tip goes inside the woman's vagina and the other can penetrate her reclining partner's anus. She sits on top and controls the thrust. If you've wondered what it's like to be a man with a penis giving pleasure to an orifice, this is close.

A male friend tells me he was in seventh heaven when he met a woman who tied him up, put a candle in his anus, and finally left him sitting on a dildo. You probably won't meet many men who would be equally thrilled, but I mention these deviations to suggest the amazing variation in what humans find sexually arousing.

Calories Don't Count

Having delicious sex in bed and on the grass, in the bathtub, on the floor, behind the green door, and on the kitchen table may make you smile more and seem even prettier. Making wonderful love may prove to be so satisfying that you'll make fewer journeys to the refrigerator in aimless frustration. And you'll get thinner. Working out daily to look neater in your divinely trashy lingerie will make you trimmer, too. But don't count on sex as an aid to calorie control.

In the most heated throes of lovemaking you can burn up to 250 calories per hour, but alas, the average person keeps up this pace only five minutes or so. That's about 20 calories, less than a small sour plum. And the passive partner may burn a pitiful 100 calories per hour, equivalent to a handful of watercress.

Dr. Gabe Mirkin, sports medicine specialist and author of *Getting Thin,* who collected these statistics, says studies done at the University of Rome show that foreplay consumes perhaps 100 calories an hour and a passionate kiss is worth 6 to 12 calories. Orgasm burns 400 calories an hour, but since most orgasms may last only fifteen to thirty-five seconds, no more than 3 calories are consumed, less than a thin asparagus spear.

Heartbeats as high as 180 per minute have been recorded, due to a rush of hormones, but increased heart rate due to circulation is what makes your heart stronger, Dr. Mirkin writes. So making love is neither a boon to the cardiovascular system nor slimming magic, but don't despair. It isn't fattening, either. The calories in an average ejaculation are truly minimal—about 30, equal to eight medium strawberries.

Keeping It Hot— When Love Is Not Enough

"What do you want to do?" she said.

"Whatever you want to do."

"I want to do whatever's best for you," she said.

"What's best for me is to please you."

"I want to make you happy, Jack."

"I'm happy when I'm pleasing you."

"I just want to do what you want me to do."

"But you please me by letting me please you," he said.

Does this sound like a loving couple debating where to go on a Saturday night? Yes, they are loving, this husband and wife from Don DeLillo's novel *White Noise*. Alas, they are in bed and the tortured politeness is about sex, their dialogue a distillation of affection and boredom.

Anyone who has ever fallen madly in love can never forget that dizzying passion—whether it lasts weeks, months, even years—the feeling of soaring, of walking on air. For liaisons that last there is a time when that passion is mingled with the warmth of intimacy and the security of attachment. The anxieties that fuel passion diminish. And there are moments in bed together when the feelings of love and tenderness are as dizzying as that wild lust once was. As the relationship matures there is a new bond, a sense of powerful commitment. And for most long-term lovers the thrill is gone or severely diminished. Many couples accept the trade-off—intimacy and commitment for intense passion—and their lovemaking is warm, familiar, affectionate, and satisfying. Others busy themselves in careers and child raising, hobbies and community service, downgrading sex to a low priority, perhaps with minimal regret. Once you give up on sex, it becomes easier to do without. If everything truly *is* more important, or for couples with diminishing sex drive, occasional lovemaking will be enough. But most of us miss the roller-coaster ride—even the weary overachievers collapsing in bed after a fourteen-hour day long to recapture the excitement and romance of courtship.

Courtship is the first Advanced Sex exercise. Make a date for sex. Send him a bright red tie, a sexy photo torn out of a girly magazine, a key to a hotel room and a card with the time you expect him to arrive—and be wearing the same chiffon and marabou negligee as the girl in the photo. Walk in the woods or the park. Sit on a bench and neck. If your home has turned into a little league hangout or a teenagers' soup kitchen, demand your adult rights. Create a romantic nest for the two of you with a lock on the door, and if anyone asks what are those moans and screams coming from your bedroom, tell them these are the sounds of love.

Shape-up is exercise two. A man who thinks his wife is attractive is a happier man. Of course he loves you, wrinkles, gray hair, flabby arms, and all. Even so, he will be thrilled by anything you do to be more beautiful. It's a dirty rotten sexist plot, but I'm afraid it's true.

Surprise him. Change the pattern. Change the place. Change your approach. Change your response. Change your style. If you've been Rebecca of Sunnybrook Farm for twenty years, you probably won't want to jump out of the closet wrapped in Saran Wrap, with a vibrator in each hand. But a subtle change might help. (See "The Uses of Indifference, Resistance, and Anger," pages 156–157.) Take him to dinner somewhere you haven't been since your earliest dating days and talk about what you'd like to try. "What would you think if I asked you to . . ."

"I think that sounds ridiculous," he might say.

"I would love to try it. I think it would free me to be naughty in a way I haven't been for years."

"It sounds like a waste of money," he says.
"Do it just once . . . do it for me."

OVERCOME THE AGE MYTH

"You should have known me when I was younger and hot for sex all
the time." The man speaking is fifty-two and he may be genuinely
worried that he is not as easily excited as he used to be or cannot get an
erection more than once a night. Or he may be fishing for a compliment,
wanting you to affirm what he likes to believe—even though it may take
more genital stimulation to arouse him today, he is twice as wonderful,
twice as knowing, sensitive, and creative a lover as he was at twenty. It
may take a little kink, a delicious erotic shock, and inspired fellatio to
ignite the spark, and sometimes a booster to keep him hard, but once he
starts he can be a master. Expectation becomes part of the reality. The
man who expects his drive to wane at forty or fifty and is already a little
bored by too-familiar rituals in bed may find his fears fulfilled. And the
man who expects to be a reliable sex machine indefinitely has a better
chance of seeing his lust unimpaired. Sex athletes and early bloomers
tend to stay sexual—perhaps because sex is more important to them
. . . or more compelling.

"I've never been as sexy as I am today." The man speaking is fifty-
four. "I was a sexual dud in my teens and twenties. Then I met a
woman who taught me everything about women and about myself. This
is the image of myself I like. My wife and I make love five or six times a
week. It's my vanity. I am married to a sexy woman and I am a sexual
man. When I see her flirting with another man and watch him coming
on to her, I want her so badly I can hardly wait to get her home."

The same intimacy, trust, and security that can freeze sex play into
predictable rituals and responses for many long-term couples can liberate others. Security frees them to be adventurous, to share fantasies,
even to pursue the dangerous and forbidden, because the commitment is
so deep and unthreatened. In a truly liberated bed, the woman is free to
be aggressive without reprisal . . . a man is free to be more passive
without question. Mature and loving lovers know that you do not need
a constant erection to please a woman. Lovemaking need not start with

physical arousal; it can start with interest—intellectual arousal or emotion. With intense and knowing foreplay, arousal will follow.

American men have a way of turning their women into mothers. It may seem cute or comforting to be his mommy sometimes. But don't fall for it. If you want to make hot love with this man forever, you want to be his mistress first, and Mommy only in moments of dire need.

If you really care about sex, give it everything you've got in your arsenal: artifice and games, sex toys and fantasy, imagination and perversity. Review all the exercises in this book—surely there are a few ideas you are only now sensual enough, confident enough, to try. Invent a few all your own.

SEX BY THE CLOCK

So it takes him longer to bounce back after orgasm now that he's grown up. He needs some sleep and has a very early morning appointment, but the emotional desire is there. Let him try the alarm-clock method practiced by a lusty but practical sexual athlete who asked to make this contribution to Eros.

He makes love. Then he sets his alarm watch to wake him in two hours. The alarm throbs. Remembering the plan, his body awakes. His caresses awaken his woman. They make love. He sets the alarm again. And so it goes. The third alarm rings fifteen minutes before he must shower for work . . . one more chance for a quick, hot connection.

Sex by the clock is not an adventure you'd want to share every night, but it certainly can eroticize your dreams and your wakings.

The Irresistible Allure of the Grownup Woman

I could write a sonnet to youth. As a longtime confessed sensualist, I know all too well the sweetness of eighteen-year-old skin. And I could write poems celebrating the bloom of twenty-five and the golden vigor of thirty. Poets, Don Juans, the culture agree. So if you don't mind, I'll save this space for an appreciation of the older woman, the grownup woman.

Every woman over thirty-nine, every woman who has been thirty-nine for several years, owes a shower of rose petals to Anatole Broyard for his extraordinary love letter to the grownup woman, "After Bloom Comes Radiance," an essay that appeared in *Town and Country* (May, 1985).

"The extraordinary man reads the narrative of the mature face and body and is excited by it. For him, the radiant woman's consciousness of herself is like sublime pornography. She knows who and what she is; she is rich in suggestion, in complicity. She is a landscape we want to inhabit while the younger woman can only be visited."

The grownup woman is "ornamented by life." The lines and scars of the years make her more human, more complex. "One of the great difficulties in the emotional life of men—especially successful men—is their inability to surrender themselves," Broyard writes. "With a woman at her peak, there's no possibility of surrender, for both partners are conquerors. Radiance, however, is an invitation to a man to give in to his feelings, a guarantee that they too will take on grace."

Yes, these brave and extraordinary men are hard to find, but you'll do better knowing that you deserve one.

Creative Fantasy

F antasy is the glorious gift of your mind to your body—the Technicolor film your imagination creates that makes you hot. It may be a romantic reverie in which the man you love sweeps you up onto the bare back of a silken white horse and plays with your breasts as you trot through a flowered meadow. Or it may be a wild porno film, an image of yourself being caressed by a dozen hands, being raped by a gang of thugs. Or it might be a flashing reel of you commanding a meek but eager young lifeguard to kneel between your legs and make you come with his mouth.

Fantasy is the erotic scenario you play in your head as you masturbate. How wonderfully accessible fantasy is. You can switch yours on anytime, anywhere (hopefully, not while you're doing brain surgery), and no one will suspect the source of your ecstatic smile.

At dinner with your man, you can silently create any imagined playlet that turns you on. You can fantasize that he is a Bulgarian spy, a psychopathic animal trainer, Burt Reynolds, or a famous cat burglar. And by the time you reach your front door your heart will be pounding, your panties will be wet, and you may have trouble resisting unzipping his pants in the vestibule.

Fantasies can be shared verbally, too. If you can bring your mate comfortably into your fantasy, the excitement doubles. Knowing what sexual games arouse him helps. "You seem very shy sitting here in the teachers' lounge, young man," you might say, knowing his favorite fantasy involves being an innocent teenager seduced by his sultry French teacher. Or "I think you have a very bad fever and there's only one cure," suggesting a steamy little "General Hospital" drama is upcoming. Or you can do a prologue to your own version of *The Story of O*, in which he will be your sex slave and you, the demanding master.

Here's a provocative dialogue between two lovers:

"Darling," says she. "That cute little waitress has followed us home from the restaurant. She wants to know if I'll share you."

"I think it's you she's really hot for," says he.

"Well, she does have a great body," she agrees. "And wonderful skin. We could have fun, the three of us."

"I'll show her how to please you," he promises.

"And I'll share your beautiful cock with her, too."

No one's there, of course, but the two of you and two vivid imaginations making you hotter. Not all your fantasies will amuse him. As easy as it can be to arouse a man, that's how quickly the wrong phrase can cool his lust. In fact, for every man or woman excited by talking while making love, there are others who will hate it. You already know how different each man's physiological chemistry is. So are his psychosexual responses. But feeling good about yourself as a sexual woman, sensitive to his temperament, you might try body language, a murmured phrase, or your choice of nightdress to signal what you have in mind with enough ambiguity so that he can respond, suggest a slight revision more erotic for him, or . . . ignore it. Remember, it's the idea he's rejecting, not you. If you've both agreed to indulge a longtime fantasy, you might describe it in a note—then both of you have time to prepare props and costumes, set down rules, agree to limits.

A report on the fantasies of 120 men and women in the *American Journal of Psychiatry* says that females fantasize sex with another partner, forced sex with a man, observing sex, idyllic encounters with unknown men, and sexual encounters with women, in that order. Men listed their favorite fantasies as replacement of established partner, forced sexual encounters with women, observing sex, sexual encounters with men, and group sex. If your fantasy stars Warren Beatty or your old homeroom teacher or Bruce Springsteen—someone distant or vague —it's probably safe to confide in your mate. But if your secret desire is your brother-in-law or your husband's boss, or in some way suggests that you find your man deficient, it might be prudent not to mention it. A fantasy you share should be one that excites you both, without leaving one of you depressed and racked with insecurity.

Here is a cast of lively characters for any number of common erotic reveries. These may be combined by classic cliché or in weirdly original combinations. Elaborate costumes are not important. In fact, they might be too funny. You can't make love if you're laughing too hard. Sex is fun. Not funny. (Well, it's funny too, but funny is warming and cozy, not hot.) Here are just a few provocative scenarios. Feel free to invent your own.

The Wild Animal Trainer tames (or is tamed) by the Wolf Gal.

The Wolf Gal and the Man Who Thinks He's a Dog play animal crackers.

The Man-Puppy is house-trained and sexually abused by the Earth Mother.

The Earth Mother is worshipped and adored and sexually indulged by the Schoolboy.

The Schoolboy is solicited and corrupted by the Prostitute.

The Prostitute is kidnapped and forced to submit to hideous indignities by the Pirate.

The Pirate is kidnapped and forced to submit to hideous indignities by the Queen.

The Queen is humiliated and dominated and learns to love the Masked Invader.

The Masked Invader has his way with the Cheerleader.

The Cheerleader has her way with the Hell's Angel.

The Hell's Angel is seduced by the tall, gangly man dressed as a French Maid.

The French Maid is punished by the Dominatrix.

The Dominatrix tries to torture the Football Player in Bondage but succumbs to his pitiful moans and they fall in love.

And are raped at knifepoint by the Pirate, the Wild Animal Trainer, and the Earth Mother, who has amnesia. And on and on . . . ad libidinum.

It is wrong to believe that sexual behavior reflects everyday behavior or even serious desires. The man aroused by fantasies of bondage or humiliation has not the slightest wish to be mistreated in real life. In fact, fantasy lets the aggressive male experience passivity and the normally gentle, easygoing man play a dominating role. In bed we can act out games we would never enjoy in actuality. That's what's so wonderful and liberating about sexual dramas, both in imagination and when acted out. You can step into any role, no matter how terrifying and fierce—you can be anyone, do anything for just a few passionate moments—and tomorrow when the alarm goes off, you climb out of bed, still the same wonderful, wholesome you you've always been.

I suppose you can let him wear your lace-edged bikinis to the office if you like. But I'd insist that he buy himself a pair all his own.

Ideally, fantasy is great when you know how to use it and regrettable only if you can't ever function sexually without it.

One Is
in the Mood,
the Other Isn't

Some people believe in total honesty. And others hedge with little white lies in the name of kindness. When you're not in the mood to make love, it scarcely matters what reason you give. The bottom line is clear: you're not in the mood. And he is. Or you're hot and he's not.

What can you do? After all, this is the man you love and cherish, a man you respect and love to please . . . or, at the very least, a loving friend you hope will be in your life for a while.

1. You can try to put yourself in the mood. You can mentally weigh what's bothering you—a headache, problems at the office, indigestion, a feeling of being exploited wherever you go—against the reality of how much you love sex (let's assume that you do—why else would you have read this far?) and how good you are in bed and how wet and hot you'll be in a few minutes if you go along with his invitation. Take an Alka-Seltzer and a hot perfumed bubble bath and maybe a drink. Then start the fantasy machine going in your head. And just do it.

2. You refuse in the most loving way. "I'd love to make love, darling, but I need to sit here and solve this problem before bedtime. So wake me twenty minutes early tomorrow morning . . . or let's plan a special champagne supper tomorrow. I'll send the kids out on a sleepaway."

3. Negotiate a compromise. "Let me finish my homework and I'll wake you when I come to bed." You might say: "I'm too distracted to make love, but let me go down on you and make that beautiful rod you're waving at me happy and you can hug me till I fall asleep." Or he might say: "Let me kiss you and make love to you with my mouth and fingers, and then, if you have the energy, perhaps you'll give me a back rub."

If you feel that you are constantly "servicing" someone whose desires conflict with your own, of course you'll be resentful and angry. As would he. But who could resist a loving offer? Sadly, not all sex flows out of love and tenderness. Some of it reflects ego hunger and narcissism. And not all rejections are simple matters of fatigue or stress. A good way to control a mate you can't control any other way is by denying sex. Turning off is a satisfying outlet for rage or resentment.

Your happiness in bed can be splintered by biorhythms that don't mesh—he likes to make love in the morning, you aren't even human till noon and want to make love at night. Or he wants to come in your mouth and the idea repels you. Or you need to be kissed constantly and he can't bear being touched. You want sex every morning and he's happy making love on Saturday. Listening to the complaints of the lovelorn, it sounds as if some of us chose exactly the mate who deprives us most. All he wants is cunnilingus. His wife won't permit it. Someone else's wife can't understand why her husband won't go down on her. I suspect some men and women seek deprivation for fear of unleashing their sexuality. Well . . . I'll leave that speculation to Freud and Dr. Brothers.

There is an art to negotiation. Here are phrases fatal to successful arbitration and phrases that could lead to comfortable compromise.

Killer Phrases	Loving Phrases
Where do you find these disgusting ideas?	I'm scared but I'll try.
I wouldn't if you paid me a million dollars.	Well, yes, I'm nervous, but you make it sound so exciting.

Killer Phrases	Loving Phrases
You must think I'm some kind of stupid slut.	If you'll help me, and be very gentle, I think I can.
Your mother would turn over in her grave if she knew what a pervert she created.	I'll try anything once.
Everyone in your family is certifiably bananas.	You're pathological, darling, but you're so cute . . . who could say no?
Even looking at that makes me want to throw up.	I think I'm getting used to this.
Just because you've got a hard-on doesn't mean I'm going to jump up and do cartwheels.	Actually, it doesn't taste as bad as I thought it would. It's probably nutritional, too.
Alice's husband doesn't get impotent every time someone else is promoted.	I feel like a slut with this sticky stuff smeared all over me, but it's actually an exciting feeling.
Do you think Paul Newman makes Joanne Woodward do those disgusting things?	Gloria Steinem would be upset seeing me tied up like this, but I must admit I could get addicted to doing nothing while you make love to me for an hour.

Talking in a relaxed moment away from the sexual battlefield may give you the information you need to decide whether what seems like a cosmic aversion is a reflection of fear or ignorance and if you two have room for a comfortable compromise. Taunting each other and trading insults before friends can only aggravate the tension. Does one of you have a deep need that cannot be met? Or are you or he nursing unvented anger that, aired, might dissolve into apology and affectionate compromise? Talk . . . and if you can't talk, find a trained and sensitive mediator. (Look in the Yellow Pages for an AASECT-Certified Sex

Therapist, or write the AASECT national office at 11 Dupont Circle, Suite 220, Washington, DC 20036, or call (202) 462-1171.) With help you might discover how far you can go together or if it's time to bail out.

Sexual Stimulants

What turns you on? Love may turn you on. Lust turns you on. Clean, ironed sheets. Watching him undress. Smelling his scent across the room turns you on. But what can you do when you're not truly turned on and yet you really want to make love—perhaps because he so clearly is in the mood . . . perhaps because he just got home after a week on the road on a day that wore you to a frazzle.

Well, I always start with a hot bath full of bubbles and a glass of champagne and a chocolate, because that's what picks me up. You might prefer a shower, freshly squeezed grapefruit juice, and peanut butter on a Ritz cracker. Here are other stimulants, for you . . . and for him when he seems interested but slightly ambivalent . . . and some you may learn to share.

DIRTY TALK

If you never talk dirty, it can be a nice little erotic shock when suddenly you do. Tell him what you want, low-down and bawdy. Tell him how it feels in the middle of the pleasure. Make him talk dirty to you. As a steady diet this can quickly get boring, but from time to time, especially if it fits into his fantasies, naughtiness from your ladylike mouth can be wildly exciting.

TELEPHONE SEX

If oral sex is a turn-on, what about aural sex? For just pennies you can find out. Dial 976-3737. In Manhattan that call costs only a quarter. The breathy, panting, baby-talking lamebrain on the recording may make you giggle or groan or even turn off. Taste in naughtiness, like any other taste, is so subjective. For a few pennies more you can dial (900) 410-1000 and hear the day's adventures of *Scarlet O,* an erotic soap opera that changes every twenty-four hours. The "sexcapades of two lusty ladies" unfold over (900) 410-2000. And you'll hear the "forbidden fantasies of a seductive nymph" on (900) 410-3000 for about fifty cents a minute, thirty-five cents each additional minute. Island natives with lesbian appetites, luscious lady barbers in a topless barbershop, strip searches of larcenous salesclerks that evolve into passionate threesomes—every call climaxes with a climax, every day, 365 days of the year. Clearly, these little stories were written to ignite the male libido, but who knows—you may feel a warming tickle too. And if you want to learn how to spin an erotic tale, you can charge the expense to education.

There are also real live women ready to fulfill a fantasy aurally. You can charge it to Visa or MasterCard—forty-two dollars to fulfill a fantasy. You might give it to your man as a valentine and eavesdrop on the other line, but if you join the conversation the price soars to sixty dollars. Phone numbers are listed in *Forum* magazine and *Screw.*

ALCOHOL AND TRANQUILIZERS

For some women a glass of wine or a tranquilizer can be disinhibiting and sexually liberating. A little can stimulate; too much can anesthetize.

MARIJUANA

Yes, it's mildly illegal, so I can't endorse it, but some people always have a small tin on hand or perhaps a rolled joint in the freezer. If grass makes you relax without putting you immediately to sleep and seems to exaggerate your sensory responses, you probably love it before bedtime. Save it for once in a while because, as great as it is to be out of your mind with sensory explosion, it is equally great to be high on your own feelings.

EROTICA

Written erotica can be highly exciting. Some women respond to highly romantic fiction—surely that is the lure of the Harlequin novel. My favorite erotica is *Blue Skies, No Candy* (I must confess I wrote it, and I never cease loving to read from it aloud). The dominance-submission themes of *The Story of O* can make the juices flow. *9½ Weeks* is a modern variation on the same theme. The censored film version gives just a hint of the novel's erotic potential. If *O* is guaranteed to make your earth move, you might also enjoy *Exit to Eden, The Claiming of Sleeping Beauty*, and *Beauty's Punishment*, all three S&M tales allegedly by the same very talented and well-known woman novelist, writing under varying noms de plume. *My Secret Life, Fanny Hill, The Pearl, Lady Chatterley's Lover*, the books of Henry Miller, Terry Southern's *Candy*, and *Lolita* are classics. My own novel, *Doctor Love*, is definitely steamy. Anaïs Nin wrote charming erotica in *Delta of Venus* and *Little Birds*.

But I can't imagine hotter pages than those of Nancy Friday's *My Secret Garden* and *Forbidden Flowers*, two collections of women's fantasies. Reading the letters to the editor in *Penthouse, Playboy*, and *Forum* can make your pulse race, too. You might try reading them aloud to each other.

PICTORIAL SPREADS IN GIRLY MAGAZINES

Traditionally it was men who responded to visual erotica and women who favored the written word. But several studies find that women today—especially the relatively emancipated college student—are as likely to be aroused by visual stimuli as men. Some women report they are turned on by the pinups in girly magazines and even more so by the pictorials of two women making love or of a man and woman in erotic play. If the feminist in you is offended by naked women touching themselves in a giant centerfold, forget I even mentioned this . . . but it can be a turn-on to share *Penthouse* or *Playboy* with your man, discussing what he finds sexy in breasts and legs, what poses make him hot . . . what he'd like to do with this or that beauty and what the two of you could do if she were to join you at this very moment. Perhaps he'll make up a thrilling story to excite both of you as he slips down under the covers to prove that your pink nether lips are as delicious as any fantasy Playmate's.

BLUE MOVIES

Porno films can be highly erotic, some films for some women, most films for many men. Porno films can also be amazingly educational. The world would be a far better place if there were as much cunnilingus in life as there is in porno flicks. A sexual stimulant (for him at least, if not for you), educational and rentable for a pittance. That's one reason you want your videotape machine right next to your bed.

Yes, porno films can be outrageously offensive—antifemale, antisex, and even antierotic. It took me two hours after seeing *Deep Throat* to get back my normal healthy, usually reliable feeling of sexuality. The classic porn film is designed for the stained-raincoat crowd, with fantasies that turn men on. But the more ambitious films, beautifully photographed and full of plot, can be funny as well as hot, and the newer porn produced by women is romantic and not at all insulting. The mechanics of organs thrusting into organs may bore you, and you may think violence is especially despicable, but you'll be surprised what scenes make your panties wet. Some women learn to enjoy porn. And even if you never love it, learn to use it. Keep an open mind. Give them an audition.

This is the clincher: porno films do turn many men on. A normal forty-year-old man capable under the best circumstances of sensitive foreplay, twelve minutes of thrusting, and one orgasm may turn into a sexual athlete under the influence of a raunchy reel. A friend of mine reports her forty-seven-year-old lover had three orgasms in forty-five minutes, inspired by a film she'd chosen especially to fit his favorite fantasy. She lost count of her own.

You two can watch together. Distractions are a real threat to sexual arousal, and pornography can help you focus on your sexual feelings, help you concentrate on the heat of the moment. But you also have the option of ignoring the flick entirely, going down on him as the heroine does the same, your back to the VCR. Yes, it may be somewhat annoying to make love to a man whose eyes are glued to the television screen as you ride his penis to sweet oblivion. Try turning the sound down, or off entirely if aural sex distracts you. Close your eyes and just go with the wonderful feelings as you make yourself come as often as you like. There are any number of delightful positions you two can assume that give him access to the screen and to your G-spot. And afterward he can fondle you and finger you where you most love to be fondled and fingered for as long as it takes for him to get hard again.

A GUIDE TO PORN FILMS WOMEN MIGHT LIKE

Some of these are porno classics, both amusing and steamy, likely to please both men and women. A few are liberated porn, with romantic sex between scenes of raunchiness, written, produced, and directed by women.

1. *Misty Beethoven.* Radley Metzger's porno variation on *My Fair Lady* is ambitious, funny, full of steamy sex and great lovemaking.
2. *The Story of Joanna.* Expensive production. Beautiful bodies. A

variation on *The Story of O,* a tale of submission and domination. You may love it more than you expect.

3. *Legend of Lady Blue.* Romantic sex alternating with rape and violence and lesbian seduction. Something for everyone.

4. *800 Fantasy Lane.* Feminists will be pleased to see that all these exquisite women are big-time real estate brokers, even though they use breasts and mouths like crazy to make a deal. Feminists won't be too happy with the S&M sequence, especially when a man takes over to show the women how it's done. Funny. And hot. An all-time favorite.

5. *Talk Dirty to Me.* An erotic variation on the *Rainmaker* tale. Starring a grownup woman hungry for sex and the sexual con man who makes her wait while he has everyone else in sight. The heat seems especially real.

6. *Debby Does Dallas.* Beautiful blonde cheerleaders are naughty in the shower room, and everywhere else.

7. *Ecstasy Girls.* Three horny young men are hired to blackmail four equally hot sisters and their even lustier aunt, porno veteran Georgina Spelvin. Needless to say, they succeed in this well-made film with high-priced production and great-looking studs.

8. *The Afternoons of Pamela Mann.* A celebration of love in an adventurous marriage after staged rape, the deflowering of a supposed virgin (male), lesbian play, and fellatio in the park in slow motion. The surprise ending reveals a sweetly romantic notion. Funny, too. Another classic.

9. *Taxi Girls.* Great-looking street girls start a cab company, provoking sabotage, rape, and other obligatory porn flick treats, with two legends of sex films, Jamie Gillis and John Holmes.

10. *Every Woman Has a Fantasy.* John Leslie does a *Tootsie*—penetrating a women's encounter group, literally and figuratively, as they explore their fantasies. Warm and funny.

11. *Christine's Secret.* Candida Royalle, one-time porn starlet turned producer, uses synthesizer music to steam up scenes of lovemaking, passionate encounters rather than mechanical acts. Very hot, as were her earlier *Femme* and *Urban Heat.*

The Uses of Indifference, Resistance, and Anger

The classic movie plot is familiar: Boy meets girl. Boy woos girl. Boy loses girl. Boy boldly, bravely, cleverly wins her back, and they live happily ever after. But imagine this plot: Boy meets girl. Boy woos girl. Boy gets girl, happily, happily, happily. There's no drama. It's scarcely a plot at all. Overcoming real and imagined resistance is what fuels romantic love—getting the frog turned back into a prince, outwitting a prissy chaperone, overcoming the curses of angry gods, finding Sleeping Beauty and figuring out how to wake her up.

Indeed, it's not only the male hormone androgen that gives men their higher sex drive, according to Dr. C. A. Tripp. It is also the psychological excitement of taking the initiative and conquering. Once all the barriers are gone, the androgen seethes but the challenge is gone. And lust wanes. *Forum* editor Philip Nobile is a favorite disciple of Dr. Tripp and recommends his book, *The Homosexual Matrix,* "a classic study of the dynamics of arousal," as must reading for heterosexuals. For a taste of the Tripp philosophy, you have only to inject a sense of resistance into your own easy intimacy. Create a barrier. Feign indifference. Surprise your mate with a gesture or approach that is guaranteed to shock.

Insist on making love when he is so angry he's not speaking to you.

Come to bed with a new perfume and a hot new nightie and cuddle into the pillow, switching off the bedlight.

"You don't want to make love?" he says.

"Talk me into it."

Press yourself against him and say, "Please don't do dirty things to me. I'm scared."

SAY: "Don't touch me like that. It's dirty."

SAY: "No. I won't take off my clothes. If you want me you'll have to figure out how to do it with my clothes on."

SAY: "No, I want to sleep with my boots on."

SAY: "Make me."

SAY: "You can't make me."

SAY: "Nothing you can do will turn me on tonight," letting him fondle and caress you while you pretend to read or sew or watch television, not responding even as you feel your body responding.

SAY: "No, I'm not coming to bed. I want to sit here on the porch swing and let the cool night air kiss me all over."

SAY: "I'm sleeping. Yes, you can make love to me if you promise not to wake me up."

SAY: "I wouldn't do that if you bound my wrists together and forced me too."

SAY: "They don't allow us to do those naughty things in the girls' dormitory."

SAY: "Do I know you from somewhere?"

Out of the
Bedroom—
Do You Dare?

f weekends in the country or summers in France or a bungalow colony are the only times you two make love away from your nuptial mattress, he may not be ready for sex in a hammock or on a sand dune or the back seat of a taxi. Perhaps you can talk about your interest in expanding your private life into public places. Start with something easy like a hot-sheet motel with rates by the hour and dirty movies in every room. Perhaps if you're more sexually playful—in limos, on airplanes, during your Sunday hike up a mountain trail—he may get excited and unzip. An easy advertisement for your interest in adventure is this page, left lying on his bedside table.

Places for Love

1. The office, his or yours.
2. A sauna that locks.
3. On the edge of the Jacuzzi or swimming pool.
4. In the conference room.
5. On the billiard table.
6. In a roomette on the *Orient Express*.

7. In the bathroom of a 747. In the adjoining reclining first-class seats of a flight, under the blankets while the movie rolls.
8. In the shower by candlelight.
9. In a dark corner of a not-too-crowded movie theater.
10. On a golfing green.
11. While sharing a booth in a porno peep show, feeding quarters to the meter to keep your space.
12. In the car at a drive-in movie.
13. On a hayride or a sleigh ride.
14. While tied to a tree in the woods behind your mountain cabin.
15. In the locker room during the big game of the year.
16. In an outrageously expensive suite at the Plaza Athenée in Paris.
17. In the baby's playpen.
18. In the fitting room while trying on expensive clothes at Saks.
19. On the stairway (nicer if it's carpeted).
20. In a huge pile of freshly cut grass.
21. In the kitchen, over the back of a chair, while everyone's waiting for dessert.
22. In an elevator.
23. In Times Square on New Year's Eve.
24. On a fur throw on the floor of a bedroom in the Box Tree Inn in Purdy, New York.
25. In a bathroom at the Excelsior in Florence, Italy, where the bath towels are thick and fluffy.
26. On the George Washington Bridge at dawn in a heavy fog.
27. While gypsies play in the next room.
28. On chairlift #8 scaling Aspen Mountain.
29. In a corridor of Madison Square Garden.
30. In a model apartment.
31. In the anteroom to your box at the Met.
32. In the men's room of your favorite restaurant.
33. In a field of daisies.
34. On a saddle in the tack room of a horse van.
35. On horseback.

Sexual Exotica— Bondage, Playful S&M, Threesomes, and Other High Kinks

Who's to say what's kinky? So far as you're concerned, perhaps this book got a little kinky back in the chapter on underwear, while another reader is still waiting for a gambit too weird to explore. Still, all of us will agree that bondage, spanking, rubber undies, and triads are advanced erotica. You may be perfectly content with dirty pillow talk and whipped cream on satin sheets. But in the name of research, here's what else is on the menu.

BONDAGE

If you are one of those women who keep *The Story of O* in a dresser drawer, hidden between your nightgowns, I don't have to tell you the erotic impact of submission and domination tales. Perhaps with the right man on the right night you might be eager to act out a submission fantasy. Certainly the idea of being bound with silken ribbons and made love to by the man of your choice for hours at a time could have a delicious appeal.

Both men and women have fantasies of forced sex. In fantasy most women imagine themselves in the passive role. But if the advertisements for professional dominatrixes in the back pages of *Screw* magazine are a barometer of sexual interests, there's a booming market out there for dominant women. A friend of mine, a legend in his crowd for sexual sadism (from playful to serious), complained to me once: "Why do all women want to be abused? I'd give anything for someone who would make me want to lick her boots."

You can't really know till you try. For some women being bound— and possibly blindfolded, too—heightens every sensation. Although couples exploring bondage often work out the limitations beforehand (interestingly, among consenting sadomasochistic players it is often the masochist who controls the game), there is still an exaggerated feeling of being totally at the aggressor's mercy, and for some men and women that is the thrill. One woman describes screaming in raw pleasure at climax and having her lover clamp his hand over her mouth. Pinned to the bed by his body, all the energy of release was forced inward; she reports an excruciating sensation that stunned her with pleasure.

So there you are in black silk stockings and lacy garter belt, or skin-tight patent leather boots, a studded leather collar perhaps—provocative garb for victim or dominatrix. Bound and forced to endure his licks and kisses, his lingering caresses as he brings you to climax, again and again. Or tickling and licking him, bringing him close to orgasm, teasing and stopping—sitting on his face, or riding him in commanding triumph till you both come.

So you think there's no way you can get your man to agree to play bondage games? Mark the cards and challenge him to a round of strip poker. When he loses, he will have to go along with your whim. Bring along bondage accessories. Here is the inventory for

A Modest Bondage and Discipline Kit

Four silk sashes or scarves you don't wear anymore
An assortment of sturdy terrycloth bathrobe sashes or clothesline
A leather belt
Vibrator and dildo

Massage oil
Feathers
Velvet-wrapped handcuffs
Leather cuffs
Metal cuffs with lock and key
Studded dog collar and detachable leash
French ticklers
Lacy black underthings
Leather cock ring
Lace-up merry widow corset
Black silk cape
Small riding crop
Knee-high shiny black boots with spike heels

Making love in leather is a passion for some couples. Try coming to bed one night in long black gloves of the finest leather. Or see how it feels when he caresses you while wearing the softest kid gloves. You may move on to leather thong bondage and calfskin bikini panties. Rubber garments are a fetish for some people, too. If you're curious, you can order the *Latex Annual* (all the latest latex fashions and gadgets) or *Centurions (The Whole Sex Fetish Catalog),* listing shoes with seven-inch stiletto heels, dungeon toys, chastity belts, bizarre movies, transvestite clothing, harnesses, Victorian corsetry, "and a bevy of new items you never knew existed." Write to Evelyn Rainbird (see page 11) for information.

PLAYFUL S&M

A playful slap on the buttocks, a rough hand tugging your head back by a hank of hair . . . nothing too serious, but for those aroused by a touch of sadism or masochistic fantasies, measured rituals of S&M can be very arousing. If the thought sends shivers of excitement straight to your arousal system, you might want to explore it voyeuristically first. Rent an S&M porn flick to play on your VCR. *The Story of Joanna* is very elegant domination. And there is a long S&M scene in *800 Fantasy Lane* that is less violent and raunchy than most, good for beginners.

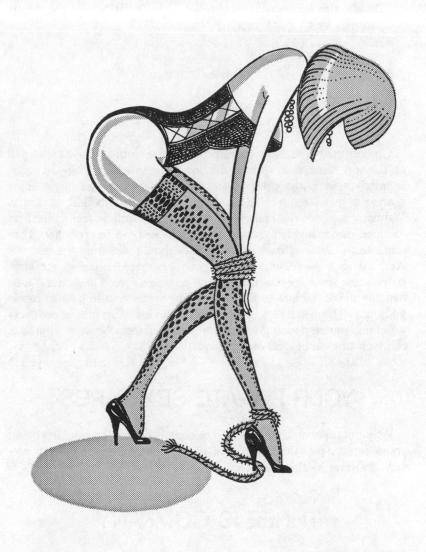

But if you just can't wait, you might try putting on something school-girlish or baby doll pajamas and greeting your man with:

"Daddy, I've been so naughty today. If I tell you what I did, please promise you won't spank me . . . too hard."

Polite Orgies

Why don't Wasps like to go to sex orgies?
They don't like to write so many thank-you letters.

On both coasts, sexually transmitted disease seems to have cast a pall on the orgy scene, even without the obligation to write thank-you notes. Infinitely safer is the effect of an orgy. The two of you might enjoy sharing a motel room with another couple you both find attractive. Watching someone else make love, hearing their sounds, feeling the heat so close, can be highly arousing. Being watched can be erotic too. Fondling and undressing each other's mates should steam up the mirrors. And all sorts of teasing foreplay can be shared: kissing, stroking, stripteasing and belly dancing, sensual massage, forced pleasuring, slow dancing naked, picnics in the raw, telling someone else how to caress your man. The mixed feelings of jealousy and lust your man experiences watching you responding to someone else's fingers between your legs can be a turn-on beyond imagination.

YOUR PRIVATE SEX TAPES

Why not capture the moment—the sounds of your lovemaking on an audio cassette—or the two of you playing out a favorite fantasy preserved forever by the video camera.

THREE IS COMPANY

Daydreaming about yourself in bed with two men or sharing a beautiful young woman with your mate, perhaps you and your best woman friend making love to your man, can be wildly exciting. Both men and women have fantasies of threesomes, imagining the endless earthly delights possible in an uninhibited triangle. For most couples, the fantasy is impossible except in vivid imagery, or on the bedroom video screen in a Technicolor sex film.

But for some twosomes the idea of bringing the fantasy into reality can become an obsession. Sharing your mate in your bed or in some anonymous hotel room is a serious emotional leap. Consider the possible scenarios carefully, and the dangers. Will you feel threatened by the adventure in some way? Do you have faith in the strength of your commitment? Are you being pressured by your love and desire to please into a scene about which you are truly ambivalent? Perhaps you are excited by the idea of watching your man thrusting into another woman, but will you freak out if he seems to enjoy kissing her? Assuming you are a responsible adult and have read my notes on pages 168–172 on sexually transmitted disease, it is most likely that your triad will star a woman, probably someone whose lifestyle you know to be without risk. If she is much younger, in better shape than you, will you be tortured with jealousy or free to enjoy the aesthetic pleasures of the moment? Are you interested in making love to a woman or merely in sharing your man with her? Would you be more relaxed at this game at home or away? What effect will this experience have on your friendship if your fantasy is a dud in reality?

There is always a potential for disappointment in acting out a fantasy that has haunted you, but some couples will tell you that occasionally sharing their bed intensifies their trust and intimacy as well as heightening passion.

The Etiquette of Sharing

Don't be too bossy (unless you've been assigned to be the General for the night).

Be sweet and clean.

Change the sheets.

If you change your mind in the middle, keep it to yourself. You need never repeat the experiment.

Your visitor is there to make sex more exciting, not to distract the two of you from each other.

Everybody has a turn.

Each has a chance to be passively pleasured like crazy.
Fetishes and aversions shall be tolerated politely.
Your man saves his only orgasm or his last orgasm for you. After all,
you *are* the hostess. But you may grant the honor to your guest.

BEDSIDE COMPANIONS—SEX TOYS

Who knows what thoughts went through your head the afternoon your Barbie doll married Ken. Growing up on Hollywood and video sitcoms, you never heard about Joni's butterfly, the secret stimulator, or the Gemini dildo with two phallic heads. Wicked as she is, you never see Joan Collins snap a velvet riding crop. But one day into your consciousness the shocking, silly, amusing, sleazy world of sex toys looms. Perhaps it was a vibrator at the drugstore that you couldn't resist buying out of curiosity. Or a Racy Underwear party in somebody's home, where you discovered Joy Jelly flavored lubricant and the ten-fingered vaginal tingler. Or did your mate buy you a Prisoner of Love kit for your birthday—with soft furry Velcro-fastened wraparounds to bind wrists and ankles and a black satin blindfold?

Manhattan is studded with little sex toy shops—the Pink Pussy Cat Boutique, the Pleasure Chest, Eve's Garden. I suspect there are similar bizarre bazaars in any big city, and all it takes to explore their offerings is the courage to walk in and the strength to keep from falling apart with laughter or disgust (depending on your perspective). Definitely you should at least try a vibrator. There is a Japanese model, sleek as the Concorde, with dual speeds and a nubby rubber wrap on the flat nose cone that is as good for deep muscle massage as it is for intense supersonic orgasms. In a sensualist's life, you'll want both.

I'm not sure how many women will love ben wa balls (Japanese women insert them so they'll feel less lonely when their mates are away). Some men enjoy the firm hug of a leather cock ring, but most will be less than thrilled. You will definitely feel better informed knowing that there are dildos that glide up and down on a piston as they pulsate (the Fantasy Stud), dildos in a cage that "turn in all directions so that every intimate area receives maximum gratification" (the French Gigolo's Secret Device), and lifelike sculpted dildos with nubby clitoral stimulators for "instant satisfaction" (the Quarterback). You may want to buy one of everything—including the glow-in-the-dark cock ring and the KY jelly lapel pin (a five-gram mini-tube). Then again, mere knowledge may be sufficient.

WARNING

It is not always simple to dispose of used or unwanted sex toys. You may not want to discard a velvet cat-o'-nine-tails or a worn-out vibrator in the trash where your sanitation man or a wandering bag lady could discover them. One couple who purchased two inflatable sex dolls—one of each gender—could not bring themselves to deflate the dolls or to stuff them into trash cans in their gossipy suburban village. The wife volunteered to take them directly to the dump—and was seen stuffing them into a trunk by a shocked neighbor in the "free wood scrap" area, who screamed as she tossed Dawn, a $49.95 "genuine pleasure slave" doll, over the edge of the dump. This is a true story.

Safe Sex
with Strangers

Remember Mr. Goodbar? The novel was based on an actual murder by a handsome stranger picked up in a West Side Manhattan bar. So there was never ever guaranteed safe sex with a stranger. And now AIDS—with all its terrifying unknowns—has made casual sex seem seriously perilous. It's true that the rising incidence of AIDS continues to be confined mainly to three high-risk groups—homosexual men, people who inject illegal drugs, and those who were infected through transfusions of blood or blood products (before routine screening of the blood supply began in mid-1985)—plus infants born to AIDS-infected women. But virologists are alarmed that AIDS is spreading to the heterosexual population. That fear has already begun to affect heterosexual behavior . . . perhaps even your own.

Scientists believe a million or more Americans have been infected by the AIDS virus and can pass it to others even when they show no signs of illness. A man can more easily infect a woman, but woman-to-man transmission has also been documented. So much is still unknown about AIDS and at what stage it becomes contagious—indeed, no one knows what percentage of seemingly heterosexual males are occasionally bisexual. But as this book goes to press, 70 percent of all AIDS cases are in New York, California, Florida, and New Jersey, making sexual contact with a person from one of these states a major risk.

If you live in Butte, Montana, or Goshen, Indiana—if you are young, if you have never been very sexually active, and live in a low-contamination area—you may have a right to feel less threatened by AIDS. If you are involved in a *totally* monogamous relationship of five or six years' duration, you can sympathize with your traumatized friends but you need not worry about your own safety.

Knowing the facts—confronting the unknowns, too—will help you decide whether you should modify your sexual behavior and what you can do.

To start at the beginning: AIDS is the final stage of an illness that is triggered by a virus. AIDS cripples the body's natural ability to fight disease. Almost all AIDS victims die, some very quickly, others within two or three years. Not everyone who becomes infected with the virus will develop AIDS. In fact, many people are infected, do not know it, and stay healthy, but appear to be able to pass along the virus, including to someone whose body cannot resist its attack.

The AIDS virus, called HTLV-III by American scientists, is fragile. It does not live well outside the body. It can be destroyed by heat, alcohol, bleach, and even soap and water. It has also been destroyed in laboratory experiments by concentrates of nonoxynol-9 at 5 percent strength—the quantity found in some spermicides, contraceptive creams and jellies sold for use with or without a diaphragm.

You do not get AIDS from donating blood. AIDS is not spread by sneezing, coughing, or being in the same room with an AIDS victim. You can hold hands or hug a friend with AIDS at no risk to yourself. AIDS is not spread by sharing a meal or even sharing a fork with someone infected by AIDS. The virus does not jump from one person to another.

AIDS is spread by sexual contact and dirty needles. (Before the virus was identified and blood donations were routinely screened, it was also spread through transfusions, a threat now virtually eliminated.) If the blood or semen of an infected person comes into direct contact with your blood, you can be infected. Theoretically all it takes is the blood or semen of an AIDS carrier coming into contact with a tiny cut or abrasion in your mouth or on the vulva or internally. No one can say how much contact is required. At this writing there has only been one documented case of AIDS antibodies in a medical worker among hundreds involved in accidental needle pricks with contaminated blood.

Rectal tissue is especially fragile. Cervical tissue is also vulnerable, and becomes extremely fragile under the influence of oral contraceptives and in pregnancy.

Drug abusers who share needles and syringes are at high risk of getting AIDS. Uncountable numbers of people who shoot drugs are already infected with the virus. They can spread the contagion by sexual contact, man to woman, woman to man. Children born to infected mothers may develop AIDS too.

You can protect yourself from exposure to AIDS.

1. Know the person you are making love to. If you are not totally confident that he does not inject drugs, that he would not have sex with a prostitute, and that he has not had a homosexual experience since 1977 . . . take the proper precautions. Abstain from vaginal and anal intercourse except with a condom and a diaphragm and spermicide containing nonoxynol-9 in 5 percent strength. Read the label carefully. Many contraceptive gels list nonoxynol-9 in much weaker concentrations.

2. Even with someone you feel confident about, you might decide to avoid anal sex and the kind of hard thrusting that could cause internal tears and abrasions. Inadequate lubrication abrades, too.

3. Even with someone you feel confident about, you may decide not to swallow semen or let it land on your face, at least till you're convinced that this man is as careful and as cautious as you are.

4. If you're losing sleep worrying that you may already be infected, see a doctor. Do not expose anyone to your blood or vaginal fluids. Use a condom and spermicide for vaginal intercourse. Do not have sex during your menstrual period.

Till now, AIDS epidemiologists and researchers have also cautioned against oral sex as a possible risk. AIDS workers have urged homosexuals to practice fellatio only with condoms and suggested that heterosexuals "not 100 percent confident about their partners" do the same. But two recent studies strongly suggest that oral sex is not a risk.

Dr. David Ostrow, a principal investigator in the National-Institute-of-Health-sponsored Multicenter AIDS Cohort Study, reports that of the 270 out of 5000 men surveyed who practiced only oral sex, not one acquired the virus over a six-month period, not even those with multiple partners.

A second two-year follow-up of 700 homosexual men with no signs of the AIDS virus in their blood found that those who practiced only oral sex—kissing, fellatio, swallowing semen—did not develop AIDS antibodies. Dr. Martin Schecter of the University of British Columbia Medical School in Vancouver, a principal investigator of the Lymphadenopathy AIDS Study reported in *Lancet* (February 15, 1986), says he is convinced that there is no risk in oral sex. Dr. Ostrow advises against swallowing semen. Dr. Schecter believes swallowing semen is not a risk. "One of the difficulties in epidemiology," Dr. Schecter points out, "is we cannot prove something never happens, but I'm convinced oral contact is not a factor in AIDS."

As we go to press, it is not clear whether the official warnings against fellatio without a condom will be revised. As a woman weighing your own risks in a new and developing relationship, you may find these two studies liberating or may want to be especially cautious until more evidence is in.

There is a strange, perhaps unrealistic, mystique among some heterosexuals—similar to that of many unwed teenage mothers. "It just can't happen to me" is the feeling. Statistics are on your side. If the man you are about to go to bed with is a healthy heterosexual male who doesn't take drugs intravenously or have sex with prostitutes, "there aren't enough zeros on your pocket calculator to indicate your chances of catching AIDS," as *Playboy* put it (June, 1985).

But if you are a woman who knows how some men shade the truth to get what they want, you may want to take precautions anyway.

You can hug and kiss, caress and stroke, play with each other, rub and come again and again—sex play without actual vaginal, oral, or anal intercourse. A whole generation of "good" girls made love that way to avoid pregnancy before the birth control pill and IUDs liberated willing hedonists. Or you can learn to use a condom. Tests commissioned by the American Foundation for AIDS Research found that condoms block the AIDS virus. Women are now buying 40 percent of the condoms sold in America.

Condoms break. But condoms used properly are less likely to break or slip. Mentor is a new condom with an applicator sheath, an adhesive that seals it to the skin, and complete instructions. Fourex are sheepskin condoms, more expensive than latex, that come in foil packets or—even safer—in tough-to-break little capsules. Some men prefer the skin because it conducts heat and feels like less of a barrier.

Here's how to put on a condom: place the rolled latex over the head of an erect penis and unroll it (retracting the foreskin if there is one) till the shaft is completely covered. Grasp the ring of the condom as you withdraw the penis so the rubber won't slip off. Never use a condom for more than one ejaculation. Don't use oil-based lubricants—Vaseline, almond oil—with a condom, because oil degenerates latex.

No one has ever made a convincing case for the condom as an erotic stimulant—though the Sexplorer, a French tickler condom with a "sexy scent," sure tries, and Japanese women use their mouths to unroll a condom on a lover's erect penis, and that could be hot.

But making love with protection is better than not making love at all. Trials of a new vaccine against AIDS are scheduled to begin late in 1986. Till the weapon to prevent AIDS chemically exists, reason may demand erotic compromise . . . for your own peace of mind if not for your very survival.

Beyond Ecstasy

A t this point, a dedicated student of *Delicious Sex* will have practiced all the exercises, tested all the recipes, rehearsed the seductive dialogue, and explored foreplans and floorplans. If you are not already a sensualist in full flower, surely the bud is ripe to burst. Obviously Little Orphan Annie does not become Brenda Starr overnight. Perhaps you are not yet quite feeling the pow of being Scheherazade, Helen of Troy, Xaviera Hollander, and Sophia Loren all rolled into one. But the seeds of the flowering are planted. If sex with your longtime mate is not equatorial, it ought to be at an encouraging simmer. And if the candlelit bubble baths and erotic massage, satin negligees, and velvet handcuffs have failed to heat up your love life, at least you're clean, you smell delicious, your skin is glowing . . . silk feels slinky against your skin . . . and perhaps a few laughs have heightened the intimacy and brought you two closer.

A dirty mind is a joy forever. But two dirty minds are hotter than one. The sex organ that really counts is your brain. Lust and animal attraction are enough for good sex. But for a satisfying sexual relationship, the ability to share thoughts and feelings about sex is crucial. Great sex with one mate forever requires art and artifice, compassion, wit, technique, and a touch of perversity. Surely you must realize it's

worth devoting as much thought and enterprise and personal invest-
ment to making love as you give without thought to your lawn, your
tennis game, and your pension plan. If you've been frustrated and dis-
satisfied for years, you can't expect to rekindle lust overnight in this
sullen, distracted roommate you once married. But most good long-
term partnerships have survived sieges of parched emotion and crisis.
It's never too late for sexual awakening, if that's what you both long for.

A friend confided to me recently that her seventy-five-year-old
mother, happily carrying on with an eighty-year-old man, had reported:
"I've never had a better lover. We meet once a week in a hotel. We hug
and kiss and then we make love, and we spend the rest of the week
recovering."

I can't imagine a more encouraging testimonial for delicious sex.
Welcome to the celebration.